Peaceful Journey

Published by Paramount Market Publishing, Inc., 2005
Copyright © 2005 by Matthew P. Binkewicz

ISBN: 0-9766973-0-0

Paramount Market Publishing, Inc.
301 South Geneva Street, Suite 109
Ithaca, NY 14850
607-275-8100
toll-free: 888-787-8100
fax: 607-275-8101
www.paramountbooks.com

Cover and book design by Mary Bolles
Cover photograph by Matthew P. Binkewicz

Additional copies of this book may be ordered from any bookstore or
directly from the publisher. Discounts for multiple copies are available
from the publisher.

Printed in the United States of America
9 8 7 6 5 4 3 2 1

Peaceful Journey

A Hospice Chaplain's Guide
to End of Life

by

Matthew P. Binkewicz

Paramount Market Publishing, Inc.

Ithaca, New York

TO THE HOSPICE PATIENTS
May their memory be eternal

Contents

Preface   *9*

What is Hospice?   *12*
The Hospice Chaplain   *16*
Millie's Prayer   *25*
Thursdays with Jesus   *35*
The General   *49*
Being Honest with Buddy   *57*
Gingerbread Lady   *72*
Letter Board   *80*
Feeding Tube Worries   *96*
Why My Husband?   *107*
Midwest Practicality   *114*
Vanessa's Dream   *130*
Epilogue   *140*

Acknowledgements   *142*
Appendix 1: A Brief Guide to Spiritual Care   *143*
References Cited   *151*

Preface

End of life frightens most of us. We find so many ways to explain away death and the dying process. When a loved one encounters a terminal illness and receives a diagnosis that signals end of life, many of us immediately enter into panic mode. We try to find "cures" or alternative treatments regardless of the facts surrounding the terminal diagnosis. In some instances, the medical community fuels our sense of helplessness and simply treats the illness while avoiding the needs and concerns of the patient and family facing end of life. It seems that we will try to avoid death at any cost.

We know from the old adage that there are at least two things that are for sure: death and taxes. So why, as we begin our new millennium, are we so unwilling to face the inevitable: some day you and I are going to die. Perhaps we view death as some sort of failure or untimely event that comes upon us with surprise. I often hear, "Had I known my loved one would have left us so suddenly, I would have done some things very differently." This phrase and countless other statements bring us to the simple conclusion: most of us spend our entire lives ignoring the signs and symptoms that a loved one is approaching the end of their earthly journey and about to embark on a new one.

Impending death brings one face to face with one's own mortality. The idea of permanent separation takes on tangible qualities that call for practical preparation as end of life approaches. A patient begins to question every aspect of life including the relationship or notion of God in one's life. Self-worth often is assigned to relationships, financial matters, and one's place in the entire universe. A logical question arises about one's life much like the one I have often heard, "What has it all been for?" A crisis, the diagnosis of a terminal illness, has entered a human being's life, and each person responds differently to this crisis.

In addition, a terminal illness, aside from the fact that it will cause death, has a profound impact upon those who are touched by it. End-of-life illness involves the patient and the family. Both are clearly affected by the dying process, and the long-term effect of the patient's death upon the family brings profound consequences that will last for many years. Dying does not exist in isolation from the rest of life. It is part of the life cycle continuum.

Death is natural to all creation. What we must overcome is our fear of the inevitable. We are all mortal, and one day we will die. The way we spend our final months, days, or hours of our lives can make a profound difference to ourselves and to those around us. Living life to its fullest until the very last moment should be the way all of us should leave this world. We should embrace our final days and not spend them in denial wondering why the medical community has failed to fix the problem or place blame on a God who is deaf to our plea for mercy.

I often compare our final days on this journey of life much like the days leading up to our entry into this world. The processes are similar in that a human being is about to embark on a journey: in the case of a newborn, the journey is along uncharted territory and for a loved one about to die, the journey will also traverse the unknown. Family and friends involved with the care of those facing end of life endure a rush of emotions. Fear and uncertainty enter everyone's life as they learn to care for the terminally ill. Unspoken moments of joy surprise both patient and family as they learn to accept death as a part of life. As the end nears, a hopeful anticipation of a peaceful repose coincides with tearful moments as a loved one begins a journey from this world into the next. Dame Cicely Saunders, the founder of the modern hospice movement, reminds her patients, "You matter because you are you, and you matter to the last moment of your life."

This book examines the lives of ordinary people facing extra-ordinary events, and the role spiritual care plays as end of life approaches. It attempts to address the hopes, fears, concerns and spiritual needs of the patients and their families as a terminal illness surfaces in a patient's life and their journey to the end. Patients and their families need to focus on the spiritual and religious issues associated with a loved one's final days. Questions of faith emerge almost immediately. Spiritual care often provides an individual with some insight into God, the dying process, and even life after death.

As the baby-boomer generation assumes the role of caregiver and in some cases, the primary care provider for an elderly parent, questions will arise in many areas of their care. This book hopes to lend support to caregivers and help address some likely spiritual issues that might arise in end-of-life care for their parents and one day, for themselves. Addressing spiritual concerns can create a peaceful end to our lives and bring a sense of hope for those who will journey on after we breathe our last. People can die without pain. People can die with great peace. People can die with great dignity. No one should settle for anything less.

What is Hospice?

"We will do all we can not only to help you die in peace,
but also to help you live until you die."
Dame Cicely Saunders
Founder of the modern Hospice movement

Hospices have been around for a very long time. Earliest evidence of hospices finds their beginnings rooted in ancient Greek civilization. Plague victims were housed in separate structures as early as the 12th century B.C. Another early account of a special facility for the dying comes to us from India around the year 225 B.C. Religious pilgrims visiting the sacred Ganges River asked the emperor for permission to die there and have their ashes scattered in the river. With the advent of the new millennium and the rise of the Christian Roman Empire, the Church assumed responsibility for establishing and maintaining hospices. Historical evidence dates as far back as the fourth century. In 325 A.D., at the First Ecumenical Council of Nicaea, a church council called by the Emperor Constantine the Great, official policy decreed that each bishop had to provide for and maintain a hospice in every city. A letter dating back to 337 A.D. and sent by the Archbishop Basil of Caesarea in the province of Cappadocia, now modern day Mara, Turkey, describes in detail the hospices built in that city.

The Christian Church continued this practice of hospice care for the sick and dying for the next 1,000 years. It reached its peak with the Crusades in the west when religious Crusader knights established hospices in Europe, the Middle East, and throughout the Mediterranean world. Other faiths soon discovered the need of hospices within their respective empires. With the rise of Islam in the seventh century, the new followers of Mohammed began to establish similar hospices throughout their empire that stretched from the Middle East along the Mediterranean Coast of North Africa and into Spain. Baghdad, Cairo, Damascus, and Cordova boasted hospices that equaled or surpassed those of their Christian counterparts.

As the Reformation took hold in the west, hospice care for the sick and the dying was transferred from religious institutions to secular ones. Monks and nuns, primarily responsible for care at the hospices, were replaced by members of the medical and scientific community. Hospices were renamed hospitals, and scientific investigation and methodology replaced the religious emphasis of faith and miracles. Throughout Europe as well as in Russia, emperors encouraged new concepts in treating diseases and promoted research and the expansion of ideas and knowledge. With the Age of Ideas and Industrialization, scientific knowledge became the leader in medical treatment. Spirituality as an integral part of person's well being was nearly abandoned. Only in a few institutions, notably Roman Catholic, was the spiritual care of an individual addressed or seen as a topic of concern.

With the advent of the 20th century, care for the terminally ill again was being addressed by concerned individuals who realized the historical as well as practical benefits of the hospice. By mid century, the growing dissatisfaction with the care being given to terminally ill patients reached its peak. Modern technology and the prevailing attitude toward patients facing end of life became untenable. Few institutions offered spiritual support as a component of a patient's overall plan of care. Hospitals and their staff viewed terminally ill patients as medical failures with whom procedures failed to cure or fix the medical ailment. An attitude of impersonal care combined with the dehumanizing effects of machines that simply maintained life without any concern for the patient's quality of life, became the norm for hundreds of thousands confined to hospitals and nursing homes. Something had to be done to stem this insidious monster from devouring all hope.

A courageous British physician, Dame Cicely Saunders established the first modern-day hospice in Devonshire, England. From this small 16-bed facility, a new wave of health-care philosophy began to sweep over England, Europe, and eventually the United States. Dignity, humane treatment, concern for pain management, and a strong emphasis on spiritual care awakened the medical world as a somewhat new way to care for those facing end of life.

Hospice work was not simply limited to accomplishing tasks, such as bathing, dressing, feeding, and medication distribution. The staff was encouraged to establish relationships with the terminally ill patients and their families. Caseloads were kept low so that nurses, social workers, and nursing aides could spend time talking with patients and their families about their feelings and experiences, or just be a supportive presence. Unlike the bureaucratic environment of hospitals with an emphasis on rules, guidelines, and procedures, the hospice movement returned attention to the care for a person. Dame Cicely Saunders writes, "It is not the illness which matters, but the person who has an illness."

Today, hospice care in the United States has become a nationwide effort to bring care and comfort to those facing a terminal illness. Over 2,200 hospices operate within the United States, Puerto Rico, and Guam offering care, comfort, and support for patients facing end-of-life illness and for their families as well. Within hospice care, the spiritual component has returned again as an integral part of a patient's overall plan of care. Spiritual care addresses the needs of a patient and family and does not engage in any proselytizing. Every faith is treated with equal respect. When spiritual care is properly administered, a patient and their loved one can find hope, peace of mind, and answers to difficult questions.

The Hospice Chaplain

"Only he who suffers can be the guide
and healer of the suffering."
Thomas Mann

Hospice guidelines specify that a patient's physical, emotional, psychological, and spiritual needs must be the focus of care. Hospice recognizes the importance of spiritual care in the overall plan of care for a patient. The historical roots of the hospice movement are deeply imbedded in the soil of religious and spiritual care providers. In Europe, care for the dying had been historically the responsibility of religious institutions. It became a part of the larger divine calling and deeply associated with works of mercy. Here in the United States, care for the dying shifted somewhat. Volunteers and professionals became spiritual care providers entrusted with the sacred work begun centuries ago by their counterparts in Europe.

Today, the hospice chaplain serves as an integral member of the interdisciplinary team. Hospice spiritual care has grown to include a wide range of religious and spiritual beliefs. A spiritual care practitioner must remove cultural barriers and practice an unconditional commitment to all spiritual traditions arising from the diverse cultures that seek this land of liberty as their home. Any notion of a dominant religious tradition should never find refuge within the care of hospice. Although the majority of patients in hospice care declare Judaism, Christianity, or Islam as their faith tradition, we must remain open and welcoming to all who come to hospice.

In the realm of spiritual care, the hospice chaplain provides a means of understanding end-of-life illness and the dying process. The journey of dying, a journey each of us will make one day, warrants a heightened awareness of a person's mortality. Normal life has been replaced by an ever-changing uncertainty as the illness proceeds and symptom management takes on more complexity. Our patients and their families need answers. They also need relief from the physical, emotional, and spiritual complexities that seem to assault them on a daily basis.

As end of life approaches, patients and their families direct their time and energy toward the spiritual realm of hospice care. Some accept death and dying as an expected event of the life cycle encouraged by the belief that heaven, the paradise of living with God in eternity, exists and awaits them in the life to come. Others find it more difficult to accept death as a part of life. Inevitably, God receives the blame for the suffering and pain that makes little, if any, sense. The question that often remains unanswered centers around one thought. "If God is just and loving and merciful, how can He allow such suffering to exist?"

Obviously there is no easy answer to the question of why suffering exists. Answers to such a question do exist, and the hospice chaplain must offer some insight into the pain and suffering that every living human experiences. The method of introducing some peace into the lives of those who suffer unresolved spiritual issues at end of life depends upon the relationship between the hospice chaplain, the patient, and the patient's family.

A family is the visible manifestation of the individuals who comprise it. As a result each individual continuously receives the projection of the family, for better or for worse, and is shaped and profoundly affected by it. Each family becomes a micro-cosm of the community. It is at once the laboratory and class-room, the battleground and sanctuary. A healthy and loving family is often recognized as a model at the heart of the com-munity. And herein lies the starting point for an effective hos-pice team approach to all levels of care at end of life, especially spiritual care: the family.

Within the Judeo-Christian framework, the traditional the-ological framework most closely associated with spirituality in the United States, the family serves as the stewards of faith, morality, and virtue. Participation in family life promotes the emergence of spiritual awareness, a sense of one's own worth and purpose. A keen spiritual awareness, developed within a strong spiritual tradition and lived out within the family con-text, allows each of us to experience our own uniqueness as individuals and our sense of belonging to the community of believers. When this is in place, spiritual care can provide answers to a host of questions, elicit more meaningful responses and dis-cussions and promote dialogue on a variety of spiritual issues including pain and suffering.

The chaplain along with the rest of the hospice team serves both the patient and family at a time of great crisis. In many cases, hospice becomes an "extended family" ready to take on the added responsibilities for providing end-of-life care, assisting the patient and family wherever possible and whenever neces-sary without trying to replace in any way, the dynamics of a good and spiritually healthy family. The goal in hospice care is to provide the best palliative care and promote spiritual, psy-chological, and emotional well being in the patient and in his or her family.

When I speak of family, I include the newest members gath-ered from the hospice team assigned to a patient. In some cases, the hospice staff serves as the only family a patient may have. We become the surrogate family and take on the role as best possible. Family can take on another layer of meaning by including the staff, whose individual members function among themselves as a family structure. If this family should experience a crisis or find itself in turmoil, then the quality of care, and the mission of hospice itself, would suffer and eventually die a spiritual death. Hospice staff, including the chaplain, needs spiritual care if they are to function at their best when they are called upon both in a crisis situation as well as in their ordinary, daily routine.

Questions about one's relationship with God arise in the mind of the patients and their families. They wrestle with spiritual issues and as end of life approaches, these issues may take on new meaning. A gifted pastor can often facilitate a discussion or dialogue about the relationship of Creator with His creation, an understanding of pain and suffering, of death and the dying process, and of the issue of life after death.

Dying is a profound rite of passage. The process takes us through mysterious and often uncharted territory. Whether in relation to Buddha, Yahweh, Allah, Jesus Christ, or another name for the Divine Creator, the hospice chaplain can serve as a fellow traveler, a companion, and guide—someone who is willing to walk along these uncharted paths with a patient and family facing end of life. Like our nurses, social workers, home health aides, and volunteers, we enter into the lives of patients and their families, and we begin to develop a relationship based on faith and trust. This relationship takes time to establish, and time is one variable that is rarely in our favor.

Yet it is our use of time that makes hospice work so rewarding. As a hospice chaplain, I try to focus the patient's energy and efforts on the present. I also encourage families to follow this approach as well. An event may arise that demands a long period of time from one or more members of the hospice team. Good use of time permits everyone involved with end-of-life care to recognize opportunities for healing.

We tend to think of time as a continuum moving along minute by minute, hour by hour, and day by day. An illusion forms that this duration is open ended, that time repeats itself. We might say to ourselves, "There's always tomorrow; let's not worry about it today." Or, "We'll get around to it." The future seems filled with possibilities and opportunities for another chance. We tend to forget about the present lost either in our past or in the emerging future.

In hospice, time must be focused on the present, the moment at hand. Patients and their families may wrestle with the past absorbed in a decade-long family conflict or denying that a conflict ever existed. Their focus may lead them to a bright and sunny future, clinging to any hope of extended life if they can just weather the present storm. Whatever the situation, hospice must insist on working in the present. We also must neither deny the past nor give up hope on the future, since both the past and the future may offer some helpful insights into the present plan of care.

Within the teachings of my faith tradition, the Orthodox Church, time—the present time—plays a crucial role. All of salvation history is expressed using the present tense. The past is made alive with prayer and song, with language that keeps a past historical event alive and present among today's believers. At the Feast of the Nativity of Christ, one hears in song, "Today, the Virgin gives birth to the Transcendent One." At Easter, the Feast of the Resurrection of Christ, we sing, "Christ is risen from the dead." In fact, throughout the liturgical year, the church incorporates her hymnody using the present tense in order to transform the past into present time.

The church actualizes time. Time becomes transfigured en-
couraging us to participate in the relationship between Creator
and creation. True time is not simply that which is assessed
mechanically by the clock and calendar. True time is living, personal, measured not by mere succession but by our intention.
Time is not just a fixed, unvarying pattern imposed upon us
from outside, but fills our lives with opportunities and moments
filled with meaning and purpose.

We can discover this when a problem is solved, a misun-
derstanding cleared up, a confession made that would ordinarily
require a tremendous amount of time. One can quietly observe
in a patient or family member the review of a lifetime accomplished redemptively in minutes. A few words or a glance or a
gesture may say it all.

We must be aware of any change. With eyes wide open and
ears attentive to the voices of our patients, we sit silently, watching for the sign or signal that a patient is ready to discuss an
important spiritual issue. If we approach them with our own
agenda or seek our own will, we will fail on all levels. The chaplain is not an expert or a source of cures and miracles. In fact,
a patient may confide in the nurse or nursing aide, someone
with whom they have come to trust not only their physical care,
but also their emotional and spiritual care as well. At best, we,
the hospice-care team, are a source of comfort, strength and hope
for the patients, their families and their friends.

Concentration, carefully developed listening, genuine openness, and commitment all contribute to the presence of the
moment. The ability to live in and respond to the presence of
the moment is an extraordinary gift with which some are born,
while in others it may develop over time. Nonetheless, it is a
gift that everyone can acquire to some extent, through discipline
and practice. Willing to share our love for our fellow human
beings we expect no compensation in return.

A regular prayer life, achieved by a process of focusing or "centering" can provide the means to reach a selfless love and concern for others. Centering involves regular meditation concentrating our efforts at the God within each of us. All too often we spend our days flying about in all directions without allowing any quiet or rest. By the time we prepare for sleep, our minds are reeling with the activities of the past day and directing energy for the tasks that await us tomorrow. We have spent little, if any, time or energy in the solitude of stillness and quiet.

Centering creates an approach toward inner reflection, giving us the quiet time we need to see and think in the present. We begin to develop a single-mindedness, the "oneness with God" that St. Paul speaks about in his epistles. Like a well disciplined gardener, we begin to cultivate the fruits of centering, inner peace, and clarity. We then can share the fruits with others offering spiritual gifts of peace, tranquility, and above all, our mere presence. An old saying among the monks of third and fourth century Egypt reminds us, "A tree often transplanted bears little fruit." A person who is constantly on the go cannot find time to be still. Without these moments of stillness, no one is able to achieve inner peace and tranquility.

The chaplain's approach must be simple and grace-filled. Honesty and respect must serve as the basis of the chaplain-patient relationship. Our calling is not to proselytize or rebuke, merely to be. On one occasion when the hospice social worker asked a patient if he would like to see a chaplain the patient replied, "Why, have I done something wrong?" At first, this may seem amusing, but it does bring out a spiritual concern for individuals facing end of life. Death brings out many feelings. Some of them have been hidden or tucked away for years. The response of the patient just quoted, is one of the spiritual issues that we need to address if we are to bring peace of mind to our patients, their families, and to society as a whole.

Hidden guilt, unresolved family matters, and questions about the meaning of life itself, can surface and overwhelm the patients and their families in their greatest time of need. An attentive ear and well trained eye, combined with compassion and intuition, can respond to the subtle nuances of the experience of those facing a terminal illness. Seemingly insignificant words and gestures may offer clues and insight into the minds and hearts of our patients and their families. Slowly, patiently, lovingly, we offer ourselves and our gifts without jumping to conclusions or leaping ahead of the person to whom we are relating. If we do, then we lose the moment, and our work may be in vain. Being a companion with someone in their spiritual journey as the end of life approaches requires us to put aside our own agendas, while accompanying those who seek our companionship and those who seek a guide along the way.

We confront the past, as well as the future, in the present. The past is approached through memory, the future through expectation. Memory and expectation operate in the present and survive as long as the individual himself survives. For something to exist in life, it has to be experienced as something in the present. Our calling is to be present with our patients and their families in order that no opportunity is missed when it presents itself.

Spiritual care consists of two important components: presence and purpose. They are not separate entities unto themselves. In many instances, they overlap. The mere presence of a chaplain can add calm to any crisis situation. Simply being a presence in someone's life can make a great difference. The purpose component, the action part of a chaplain's role, involves prayer, the implementation of sacraments including, confession, communion, and holy anointing, counseling, and developing a relationship with the patient and family.

The following chapters will yield some insight into the two components of spiritual care. Each of us can offer our presence and our purpose if we wish. All that limits us is our desire to make a difference in the life of a loved one, friend, or stranger. We are all called to serve the spiritual needs. We do not need a white collar or degree in theology. We need an open heart, an unclouded mind, and a soul filled with love.

Millie's Prayer

"Just being able to pray helps, whether your prayer
changes the world outside you or not."
Rabbi Harold Kushner.

"Matthew, do we pray for a cure to our illnesses and an
end to our struggles, or do we pray to be healed from
those things that cause us harm?" Millie asked her question with
a wide smile and angelic look. It was the same smile and look
that greeted me each and every time I visited with her. Like a
wise elder from the village or a prophet from biblical times, she
knew the answer to this question. She had developed a life of
prayer over a span of 80 years and found consolation in prayer
alone, a prayer that gave her hope, strength, and commitment to
live a life of love, a life of peace, and a life of praise.

Millie was born in the South at a time of great change in
our country. Being of African-American heritage, she suffered
much at the limitations of Jim Crow Laws and the phrase "separate but equal." Separate, yes, but equality would be a dream
only realized many years later. Nonetheless, she endured and rose
out of the pain and poverty and moved to Washington, D. C.
Having succeeded in obtaining a job and working long hours,
Millie purchased her very own home and raised a daughter.

As the years went by, Millie became a role model for many
in the African-American community. Although a keen business

person and well-liked by everyone in the neighborhood, it was her faith in God that drew so many to visit with and learn from this amazing woman. Millie was Roman Catholic, a convert to a faith that was quite alien to the majority of African Americans. She maintained a very charismatic way of praying and reciting scripture, but always had her weekly missal near her bed. In fact, one of my first assignments was to find the large print edition for her so that she could follow the daily scripture readings. Heart disease had made it nearly impossible for her to leave her home, so the church came to her.

"Millie, I think prayer can cure, but above all, prayer is the means by which we draw closer to God. And if anyone draws closer to God, then we certainly can be healed from all that afflicts us." As I finished my sentence, Millie closed her eyes very tightly and gripped my hand. We sat silently for a few moments, though it seemed much longer.

She broke the silence with an impassioned plea and with tears beginning to flow down her cheeks, "Then let's pray, because I don't want to be far from my God."

∞

Prayer is the universal presence of God's love for His creation. Prayer is our spiritual link and a window into the life of faith. It unites us with our Creator and unites us to each other. Prayers are threads of the very fabric that are woven within each person to make a garment that becomes our spiritual life. Prayer is the most versatile tool that we have in end-of-life care. Everyone can use it whenever and wherever they wish.

The Orthodox Church possesses a deep prayerful life and offers her worshippers a wide opportunity for both communal and private prayers. The Divine Liturgy, or more commonly known among western Christians as the Mass, provides the faithful with the highest form of prayer—worship of God within the sacrament of the Holy Eucharist. Orthodox Christians pride themselves on the number of services taken in church as well as in the homes of the faithful. Walk into most Orthodox Christian homes, and you will find an icon corner situated in the main room of the house where a family prays together. In each bedroom, you may find a smaller version of the icon corner where one may pray in silence and in obedience to our Lord's command, "When you pray, go into your room, and when you have shut the door, pray to your Father." (Mt 6:6)

Prayer is personal while at the same time prayer is communal. Many travel to houses of worship every week to offer praise to God. They stand, sit, and kneel to offer prayer and song. Even though many gather together to worship as a community on their day dedicated to God, each person also offers prayers that are personal and specifically intended for God's ears only. Whatever name we call upon, prayer provides the vehicle, the method of transmission of a hope, a desire, or some need that can and must bring about some transformation in our life.

For those of us in hospice, prayer is often a means by which we can begin to understand our patients and their families— their struggles, their hopes, their fears, and their dreams—as they prepare for the end of their journeys on earth. What surprised me most during my first few months as a hospice chaplain was the surprisingly high number of patients, and to a certain extent, their immediate families, who had grown up without a tradition of private prayer. When the topic of conversation veered toward prayer and the frequency of daily prayer, most admitted that they had never given much thought to prayer outside of church.

It seemed that prayer was a mystery to many. Some stated that they had no idea what words to speak in prayer except for the ones they learned as children, such as the "Our Father" and "Now, I lay me down to sleep." Some claimed they had never been given any instruction on how to pray. A few even doubted that their prayer would be heard by God seeing as He must be busy with more important requests than theirs or that they were not worthy to be granted what they sought in their prayers. Others mistakenly believed that their efforts would be futile. In a world that seemed to be more materialistic and less spiritual, why would any God listen to the voice of some one preparing to leave this world.

Despite all of these testimonies, the patients and families that I met longed for prayer. Deep within, they sought some method, some means by which they might be able to pray to God with a regularity and familiarity that seemed to have evaded them for most of their lives. After a lengthy discussion about prayer, one family member whispered in my ear, "If I could pray like Grandma, I know my life would be different." Like this individual, many of us have been touched on a personal level by a particular person we know who has been made who they are by their trust in prayer. As I probed further about "Grandma," I discovered she was a tremendously courageous woman who struggled her whole life with poverty, illiteracy, and racism. With every battle she faced, she found comfort in prayer.

For those who have a longing for prayer and yet have never prayed, I offer my understanding of prayer. Prayer is conversation with God. It is our channel of communication between Creator and creation. God brings all of humanity into existence through love and makes us in His image. This single act of love flows into all of creation and gives meaning to everything both visible and invisible. In the Old Testament, the word for God's love in Hebrew, *chesed*, is used 185 times while the New Testament mentions God's love in Greek, *agape*, 138 times.

God's love is best likened to a mother's love for her newborn baby. She watches over the child, observes the cries and other noises, and attends to the needs even though the baby is incapable of communicating his or her needs. This same love continues throughout the developing years of the child whether or not that child disappoints, frustrates, or brings joy to the mother.

God's love is always there for us whether we feel it or not. There is no diminution of His love depending upon our state of mind or what others may think of us. It is an unconditional love, infinite, and does not depend upon our "good behavior." No matter how skewed we become or how far off the mark we may fall, God is there for us, always willing to hear our prayers, to extend His love to us. The thief who was crucified with Christ demonstrates this most vividly when he repents and asks Christ for forgiveness. (Lk 23:39–43)

This means that no matter how thoughtless or even depraved a person may seem, because of the persistent presence of the image of God, there is a basic goodness in every human being that connects us to God and to one another as well. Therefore, prayer to God is always acceptable and does not depend upon preconditions or a set standard of behavior.

The presence of God in each of us makes prayer possible. The power of prayer is related directly to the idea that each of us is created in the image of God. This shared image of God allows us to pray and to love God and each other. Our act of love, of care, and concern for our fellow brothers and sisters is a manifestation of prayer. When a loved one enters the final days of life, prayer can be a welcome relief for the patient as well as the family. Prayer often can alleviate the fear and uncertainty a patient and family experiences as death approaches. Prayer, one of those little things that we take for granted, can make a positive difference in the healing process for all involved.

The special bond of love that exists between us and God centers around prayer. Prayer brings healing, and that notion of healing provides hope to a person who faces a terminal illness.

And, the family also finds hope knowing that a loved one leaves this life with consolation, a sense of meaning, and some degree of fulfillment. For in God, all things are finally healed. Some of the healing will be completed in ways we cannot know, in the true "mystery" of prayer and its real power to effect change.

There is no correct way to pray. Prayer is an expression of each person's relationship with God. Each of us is unique, and our prayer is unique. As we learn to pray we are finding a method of prayer that suits us in a particular way. If you are someone who is praying for the first time, you must find what suits you best. This does not mean that you have to reinvent the wheel. There are many wonderful prayers and books devoted to prayer. Scripture reminds us that the most important prayer is the one taught by Christ, the "Our Father." (Mt 6:9–13).

As we grow and mature, we change and so do the people around us. Events in our lives are constantly changing, and as they change our prayer life also changes. Because our life of prayer with God is an ongoing relationship, we need to understand that our prayer is going to change according to what is happening in our life. With Millie, the woman mentioned earlier, the struggle with prayer had taken on a complicated twist. She had to make sense of her own terminal illness, the start of her own journey toward the end of life, and her daughter's struggles as the primary caregiver.

Life is often very complicated. Crises seem to come in waves, not as a single isolated event that waits patiently for a resolution. Millie was worried about her prayer. Would God think her too selfish if she spent time on her concerns rather than on her daughter's crisis? The peace that prayer once brought to her seemed illusive. She expected prayer to always be the same. Yet she learned slowly that prayer was dynamic, not static. It evolves in our lives, leading one closer to God while at times taking us over some rough terrain.

As in any relationship, the effort one must put into it to have a successful outcome is tremendous. The same is true with a life of prayer. Prayer can be difficult. Our relationship with God in prayer is not a one-way street. God willingly listens to our prayers and pours out His love, but He expects some effort on our part. We must be willing to put in the time for prayer. God's grace is superabundant, but it is not to be taken for granted. When we pray, we might not receive what we want when we want it. Results are rarely instantaneous. Sometimes, they are barely perceptible.

Since prayer does not always produce evidence of some benefit when needed, our society looks to it as unimportant. Why spend time every day doing something that many claim has great value, that offers healing, yet is not measurably productive. In our modern world, emphasis is placed on productivity. If someone is not productive, they are regarded as less: the old, the infirm, the handicapped, the homeless, and the poor. We seem to have missed the mark.

Prayer can be highly productive, but it takes time. Above all, we need to incorporate a time and place each and every day for prayer. For some, it will be the morning quiet after the children leave for school. Others may choose the evening when most are preparing for bed. A few may take a minute or two throughout the day and offer up a short prayer or moment of reflection. The key to a good and faithful prayer life is to keep it within the limit of your ability.

What impressed me most about Mille were not so much the words she used, but rather how she prayed—her attitude, her beliefs, and her constant struggle with prayer. She too, became discouraged and dissatisfied with prayer at various times throughout her life. Often, she did not get what she prayed for when she wanted it. The answer to her prayers did come, but it was not on her time. Many times she found herself dozing in prayer, and even bored by it. Yet, each time adversity or prosperity came to her home or her family, she turned to prayer. In times of joy as well as in times of sorrow, she had a prayer. She had confidence and deeply believed that prayer was one way to share a life of love with God, a lifetime of discovery and re-discovery in an ever changing world.

When a person receives a diagnosis that they have six months or less to live, profound emotional and spiritual issues arise. Patients, their family members, and their friends all respond differently. Fear, anger, hope, frustration, and faith all play a role as a person's final days approach. For some the atmosphere of uncertainty tests the limits of faith. Yet this same uncertainty creates an opportune time for prayer. Regardless of the time of day or where they might be, prayer is the first weapon in spiritual combat.

What individuals might ask for in prayer varies greatly. Patients may pray for a quick and painless end. Caregivers, close family members and friends, may pray for just a little more time, just one or two more days to finish the work that needs to be done. Dying is not a passive process. Dying takes time. Dying takes energy. Dying requires so much from so many. In prayer, the patient, the family, and even the hospice staff can find relief, can sustain their vigil, and can find hope where there was once no relief, no hope.

Millie has been in hospice for nearly two years. She was diagnosed with congestive heart failure (CHF), and her physician explained the situation to her with great compassion. He offered the possibility of hospice, and Millie thought it was a good start. She agreed with the philosophy and was prepared for the final months or weeks that remained.

A year and a half have passed since her initial meeting with our hospice staff. At once, each on the hospice team was charmed by Millie's gracious and sincere personality. The social worker, the nurse, and I, her chaplain, instantly fell in love with this woman. Her honesty, her spirit for life, and her total acceptance of God's will in all things gave us courage, provided us with hope, and on many tough days, sustained us in our never-ending routine of caring for those facing terminal illness.

Millie prayed daily. When she could not find the right words, she turned to scripture, especially the Psalms. She once said to me, "The Lord read the Psalms, and that's good enough for me." She smiled as she finished her sentence and then asked me to join her in prayer. The following is a prayer she recited with me. I share it with you so that you might find comfort knowing that prayer comes from the heart, where our love for God and each other resides.

Lord, thank you for the gift of life you give me every day.
Lord, thank you for the wonderful people you bring to me.
Lord, thank you for the hospice that comes to visit.
Lord, thank you for people who protect our nation.
Lord, thank you for the family and friends who stop by.
Lord, thank you for our leaders who do their best every day.
Lord, thank you for your love.
Lord, thank you for the social worker.
Lord, thank you for the nurse and the aide.
Lord, thank you for the chaplain and all the ministers.
Lord, thank you for Your Mother, a Mother to us all.
Lord, thank you for the illness, so that I may learn love.
Lord, thank you for the times you visited, though I didn't know it.
Lord, thank you for the blessings you granted, though I didn't deserve it.
Lord, thank you for the joys of my grandchildren, they are my treasure.
Lord, thank you for strength when I am weak.

Lord, thank you for hope when I can find none.
Lord, thank you for faith when I doubt.
Lord, thank you for never growing tired of my voice.
Lord, thank you for your mercy when I fell short.
Lord, thank you for being there when I was alone.
Lord, thank you for seeing me through the tough times.
Lord, thank you for a life of love and triumph.
Lord, thank you for everything, everything, everything.
Amen.

Thursdays with Jesus

"To everything there is a season, and a time
to every purpose under heaven."
(*Ecclesiastes 3:1*)

One afternoon, in late December, Shelia, a hospice nurse, informed me of a new patient in one of the local nursing homes. The patient, a 92-year-old woman, was admitted to the program with a terminal diagnosis. "Matthew, she is going fast, and you better get right over there." She spoke these words having just finished the hospice admission paperwork at the nursing home where the new patient had been transferred. With Shelia's urgent request, I drove to the nursing home. Hospice nurses are very special people, and I trust their instincts in assessing many end-of-life situations. Nurses, along with the other members of the hospice-care team, are like angels, and the care they provide is truly a gift from above.

Sarah, our new patient, had neither family nor friends. Never married, she had lived her entire adult life alone. No relative or friend could be found. She had kept to herself for many years. One day a neighbor remarked to the mail carrier that she had not seen Sarah for several days. Meanwhile the mail carrier noticed the mail piling up in her mailbox and suspected that something might have happened behind the closed doors of

Sarah's home. A call was made. The paramedics arrived along with a police officer. They entered her home, finding her in a weakened state, unable to get out of bed. The ambulance transported her to the nursing facility, where the staff determined she was severely dehydrated, confused, weak, and by all indications, only a few days from leaving this world.

It is a sad fact that, hospice professionals frequently come across elderly people living alone with little if any family support. Changes in the family structure have compromised the way we care for our elderly family members. Children and grandchildren now live hundreds and even thousands of miles from parents and grandparents. Greater mobility and increased employment opportunities nationwide mean new careers and promises of greater economic freedom. Family members, many of them the logical caregivers to elderly parents, make difficult choices as they pursue their own dreams. These choices often place greater distances between family members. The traditional role of children as caretakers and primary-care providers for their aging parents is slowly disappearing in our rapidly mobile society.

A terminal illness adds an even deeper layer of concern for the patient and for family members as their care providers. Elderly parents fear becoming a burden to their children as the terminal diagnosis necessarily alters everyone's lifestyle. Care for a loved one will demand more time and resources. Families will need to sit down and outline the kind of care a loved one needs or has requested. Many questions will arise concerning the plan of care especially when deciding between aggressive measures to treat a terminal illness or to simply provide care and comfort as a loved one faces end of life.

Family members who are the care providers for aging parents find themselves stretched to the limit as an avalanche of information comes their way. In some instances, care providers will be asked to make decisions on matters that they themselves have not discussed with a terminally ill patient, such as the medical care someone desires, or even whether the patient is capable of making a decision. This medical directive, called an "advanced medical directive" enables individuals to spell out just how much or how little medical treatment they wish, should they become incapable of communicating their wishes.

For example, should a feeding tube be inserted if a loved one loses the ability to swallow or should comfort measures be set in place to ensure a peaceful and pain-free end of life? Should the patient be placed on a ventilator if normal breathing becomes impossible, or should comfort measures be employed to guarantee a painless and comfortable death? Perhaps cardiopulmonary resuscitation (CPR) should be started if the heart stops beating; or would a "Do not resuscitate" (DNR) order be more in line with a loved one's desire to end life naturally without any unnecessary prolonged treatment? Added to these concerns are the emotional and spiritual needs confronting a family as a loved one slowly prepares for their journey from this earthly life.

Most of us are unprepared for this daunting task. When asked to make these decisions with or for our loved ones, the process easily becomes overwhelming. Few of us have sat down with our care providers and discussed our own advanced medical directives should we be diagnosed with a terminal illness and find ourselves unable to communicate our wishes. A dying person will often say, "Let my children decide; they know what's best for me." Such a person's children can become overwhelmed with guilt, confusion, anger, and feelings of helplessness as they must decide whether to give or withhold treatment. These are serious issues that need to be addressed before a crisis occurs.

If a patient comes to hospice without family, friends or without any advance directives or medical wishes concerning end-of-life care, the nursing facility, hospice, and the state-appointed legal guardian automatically become the care providers. They are responsible for making health-care decisions based upon state and national guidelines. This was just the scenario for Sarah. Medical care would be administered based upon the nursing-home physician's directives and in consultation with hospice, since she had neither any living relatives nor friends, nor did she have written instructions for end-of-life care. It was clear from the doctor's diagnosis that she would not be with us for very long.

I entered the room, and looked upon the frail woman lying in the bed. A small amount of sunlight filtered into the sterile surroundings and created a surprisingly peaceful atmosphere. Sarah's hair was as white as snow and combed straight back. Her face, ashen and dull, showed her age as well as the recent months of silent, interior struggle and decline. As I approached the bed and gently called her name, there was no response. Her breathing appeared to have stopped; I wondered if I had arrived too late. But on closer examination, I could see a faint rise and fall of her chest under the thin white sheet. She was indeed alive, barely, but alive. I sighed with some relief, and I moved closer to her bed. Again, I looked at her face. It was a face that told a story of a life lived by a woman on her own for many years.

Drawing just near enough, I gently called out her name. She awoke, somewhat startled to see my face so close to hers, and asked, "Who are you?" I replied, "My name is Matthew, and I am the hospice chaplain." With a look of great relief, she said, "You've finally arrived. Would you mind saying a prayer? But then you'll have to leave. I've had a full day of visitors, and I am so very tired." She finished her last sentence with a deep, somewhat painful sigh, much like a marathon runner crossing the finish line.

I stood by her bed completely surprised by her response as well as her ability to say several coherent sentences. I said a prayer with her, and she smiled, managed a barely audible thank you, and closed her eyes. I left the room and wandered back to the nurses' station wondering why the initial report painted such a bleak outlook for our newest patient. I spoke with the head nurse, and she reiterated Sarah's condition upon her arrival to the facility. She had suffered severe dehydration, and in her weakened condition, appeared to be on her way out. However, with an intravenous solution to build up her fluids and electrolytes, Sarah slowly began to gain her physical strength and mental capacity within hours of her arrival.

Sarah improved over the following months. Although her terminal diagnosis remained, she slowly began to regain some strength. The doctor ordered that her diet be changed from thickened liquids and pureed foods to a normal one since she had regained her strength to chew and swallow. Often a physician will order a special diet to prevent any possible aspiration of food or liquids into the lungs. When aspiration does happen, it often results in pneumonia and complicates a patient's delicate balance between life and death.

As she regained her stamina, other signs indicated a change in Sarah's condition. Her conversation grew livelier with time, and she won over the hearts of the nursing home staff as well as our hospice team. One member of the nursing home staff, Sally, had grown especially fond of Sarah—charmed by her subtle wit and affection. Our patient had reached the level of pleasant forgetfulness peppered with an occasional outburst of sobbing or laughing depending upon her emotional state at the moment.

On a particularly beautiful afternoon, I paid a visit to Sarah. Sally, the floor nurse, stood at the bedside massaging her feet with lotion. What kind acts of mercy the human race can perform when given the chance. I marveled at this scene. Any stranger would think the nurse was Sarah's daughter. As I entered the room, Sarah looked up, smiled, and said, "Look, its Jesus," Sarah said with a smile beaming from ear to ear as I entered the room. She continued her thought, "He visits me every Thursday." The smile remained on her face which radiated warmth and sincerity that words fail to capture. Sarah, our 92-year-old patient was a woman of deep faith and had experienced much over nine decades.

After a few minutes of general pleasantries, I asked her if she really thought that I was Jesus. Now I must tell you that I have long reddish brown hair tied back and a reddish brown beard to match. Perhaps, with her condition and her memory setback, she might have thought that I was indeed Jesus. She smiled, blew me a kiss, and replied, "You visit me and pray with me. Isn't that what Jesus told us to do?"

She patiently waited for a response. I looked her straight in the eyes and said, "I guess we are all Jesus, especially when we visit those in need or spend some time with someone."

Sarah looked intently into my eyes as her own filled with tears. As they slowly rolled down her wrinkled cheeks like water tracing its way down a well-worn hillside, she spoke with child-like simplicity, "My mother is in the next room and there is no one to take me to see her." Her tears continued to flow. I gently took her hand into mine and spoke some simple words of comfort reassuring her that she would see her mother.

∞

While listening to Sarah, I was reminded of my own grandparents and their generation. As a child growing up in the southern tier of New York State I was surrounded by immigrant grandparents and myriads of older relatives who spoke for hours about their lives in Eastern Slovakia, Poland, and Ukraine. One aspect of their lives remained constant: their deep faith in God. No matter what had happened—world wars, the Great Depression, prejudices, or ill health—each story ended with an account of how their faith had gotten them through the rough times. I marveled at these elderly people with round smiling faces who spoke in thickly accented English reminding young and old alike of God's mercy and love. Faith had been a stabilizing force in their lives. On Sundays they often quoted parables from the Gospel that had been heard during the Divine Liturgy. Their words echoed in my mind. I marveled at these wise elders who seemed to solve all problems with their deep faith and love for God and for each other. Raised with this tradition, I soon found my own solace and comfort in the Gospels of the New Testament. Within these pages, one can discover and rediscover eternal truths. All the virtues of humanity—charity, hope, faith, humility, etc.—are described in biblical parables teaching us to live a life of love, compassion, understanding, and peace.

It is said that parents unconsciously name their children after those whom they wish them to emulate, as they grow to maturity. From what I know of St. Matthew's life and writings, I see myself reflected in his way of thinking, his mannerisms, and his deep faith in Christ. It is not surprising that my favorite Gospel is attributed to this apostle and evangelist.

If you spend some time with The Gospel According to St. Matthew, you hear a powerfully moving account of humanity's role in the divine plan of salvation. In Matthew 25, Jesus Christ is with His disciples at the end of His earthly ministry. Knowing that His own death is certain, Jesus instructs them that faith must be put into action. Good deeds and works of mercy need to accompany their thoughts and their words. The Christian faith, Christ's teachings, are a vital part of every day. The following exerpt from Matthew's Gospel can illustrate the importance of a faith being translated into action.

"Come, O blessed of my Father, inherit the kingdom prepared for you from the foundations of the world; for I was hungry and you gave me food, I was thirsty, and you gave me drink, I was a stranger and you welcomed me, I was naked, and you clothed me, I was sick and you visited me, I was in prison, and you visited me." Then the righteous will answer Him saying, "Lord, when did we see You hungry and feed You, or thirsty and give You to drink? When did we see You a stranger and take You in, or naked and cloth You? And when did we see You sick or in prison, and come to You?" And the King will answer and say to them, "Assuredly, I say to you in as much as you did it to the least of these My brethren, you did it to Me." (Mt 25:36–40)

The Gospel account urges us to attend to this: For any Christian aspiring to an authentic life of discipleship, hoping to enter into the Kingdom of Heaven, those who are in need must be a priority. If we fail to serve the least among humanity, we will find ourselves excluded from eternal life in paradise.

The message of this Gospel passage clearly illustrates Christ's teaching to His disciples then and now: To be like Christ and find the true meaning of living a life of faith in Him—filled with love, compassion, and understanding toward our friends and even total strangers—we need to put our faith into real action. We ought to devote a significant amount of time, energy, and resources to those in need, regardless of the circumstances that placed them in their current state of need.

True faith must be unconditional. Both friend and stranger, and even our enemy, are seen as an image of Christ. In my faith tradition, the Eastern Orthodox Church, our theology is firmly planted in the belief that all humans are created in the image and likeness of God. From the story of creation in the book of Genesis, we see the first evidence linking human existence expressed as an image of God. "Let us make man in our image and according to our likeness." (Gn 1:6) This statement brings out two important theological concepts. First, God speaks to His people in the plural voice. The words, "Let us make," signify a plurality of persons in the Divine Godhead. The Trinity—Father, Son, and Holy Spirit—work together in their creative act. Love unites the three persons, who are one in essence. They cooperate with mutual love and mutual respect.

The love of God as expressed in the three persons of the Holy Trinity flows into all creation, and this is the second theological concept contained within the words from Genesis 1:6. We human beings are the crown of God's creation, and we hold a unique position in the cosmos. The doctrine of the Trinity is not simply a theological statement. It is a call to action in our daily lives. Since we are made in the image and likeness of God, we are called to live the Trinitarian life of mutual love and mutual respect of heaven here on earth.

Humans are the physical, emotional, and spiritual manifestation of God's limitless love. The Divine image is made manifest in each person composed of body, soul, and spirit. No other creature bears God's image and likeness. We humans are in every sense truly capable of knowing right from wrong and are endowed with the greatest distinguishable trait, free will. This trait of free will is essential for an understanding of human beings made in God's image. Because God is free, we are free. With this freedom, each of us actualizes the divine image within ourself.

People are not merely mechanical creations with replaceable parts like some machine. Each of us is unique, one of a kind, and cannot be re-created or mass produced. As there are some 4.5 billion people living on this planet, so there are 4.5 billion distinct and unique images of God. All of us are equal in His eyes. God has no system by which humans can be measured to be of more or less value than another. Quantitative values are meaningless to humans made in the image of God. A Wall Street lawyer and a beggar in India, though very different outwardly and judged by some in society according to worth or earning potential, are nonetheless equal in the sight of God.

By receiving the influx of God's love we must allow this love to flow to our brothers and sisters who cry out in need. Humans, made in the image and likeness of God, are bound to an awareness of the needs of fellow brothers and sisters. If we remove God from the relationship, we no longer can be called human beings. Men and women become objects rather than subjects, replaceable, commodities with the unthinkable value judgment that one person is of more worth than another. We need to learn to let God love through us—to love as He loves.

History has shown the unthinkable nightmare a living reality. Since the Industrial Revolution an increase in secularism has led to a growing dehumanization of society. Lenin's rise to power in Russia and the brutality of the communist regime under Stalin demonstrated how the denial of God lead to the cruelest repression of humanity placing value on some persons and labeling other as "expendable" and even worse, as "to be eliminated." Nazi Germany, Fascist Japan and Italy followed in the same pathway torturing and executing millions based on their value in a society which did not recognize all persons as being made in the image and likeness of God.

Human beings became expendable commodities, and nations began to follow unthinkable plans of "ethnic cleansing" entire populations. These tragic practices continue today in Africa, the Middle East, and Asia, as political systems, bereft of any idea that humans are created in the image of God, decide who is of value and who is expendable, unwanted or an easy scapegoat for economic and social problems.

The only faith stance that can secure human freedom and dignity lies within the conviction that each of us is created in the image of God. Our relationship with God takes on deeper layers of meaning since the Divine image in each of us links all of humanity together. Being united with each other through this inter-communion with God and intra-communion with our fellow human beings transforms the quality of human relationships. When we suffer, we do not suffer alone, but all of humanity hears our cry and shares in our pain and suffering. The reverse is also true: our joy and prosperity are justified only when others can be joyful and celebrate, too. Faith compels us to struggle at every level against all forms of oppression, selfishness, and violence.

∞

Sarah lay in her bed. She was like thousands, if not millions, of elderly people facing a terminal illness. During my visits with her, she often recalled her years as a young girl in Cumberland, Maryland. "I could milk a cow faster than any of my cousins, so Granddad let me milk the cow ahead of all the rest. And I'm not going to tell anyone how to do it." She continued to describe in vivid detail life on her Granddad's farm in western Maryland.

My mind painted pictures of a horse-drawn plow breaking up the earth into neat furrows. Following behind the plow and

Granddad was Sarah, gently placing corn or wheat or some seed into the newly opened soil. Both of us enjoyed the trip back in time. In that bed I saw more clearly than ever the Divine image in humanity. Sarah's lifetime of living was sacred. Although she was now restricted to a bed and dependent upon others for her daily needs, she was still a person, fully alive, bearing the image of the Divine, shining as brightly as the day she was born.

We hear many stories from our patients. They are bits and pieces of lives filled with joy and sorrow, goodness and concern, pain and hope. In many ways, these folks, awaiting the end, are just like us. Each of them has a story to share, a life they wish to retell to anyone who will take time to listen. In Viktor Frankl's famous book, *Man's Search for Meaning*, he goes to great length to explain the importance of all that we experience in life, especially suffering and pain. "What you have experienced, no power on earth can take from you." Life is filled with experiences. Our thoughts, words, and actions make us human. Human life never ceases to have meaning and includes suffering, dying, and death itself. Nothing is lost even though it may be a part of our past.

For Sarah, her recollection of life on a farm nearly 80 years ago was her greatest possession. It provided her with an identity, a way of expressing to others who she was and how she now saw herself. Deep inside each of us, we know there is some one we were meant to be. And we can feel when we are becoming that person. The reverse is also true. We know when something is off, and we are not the person we once knew. Whether we recognize it or not, we are all on a quest for answers, trying to find meaning in this very short journey we call life.

We all wrestle with fear and guilt in our search for meaning. We seek to discover who we are and how we can become truly happy, truly fulfilled. By simply living through the course of a lifetime, people like Sarah learn many lessons of life.

Although they might not have found perfect happiness, power, or wealth, they are at peace with themselves. The lessons we learn on this brief journey of life are not about making life perfect. Rather, it is seeing life as it was meant to be. As one patient so eloquently stated as his own body refused to obey his mind's commands, "I find great joy in the imperfections of life."

By the time we meet our patients, they have but a few months to live. Some find themselves in unfamiliar places. They might not live in the town where they were raised, attended school, lived and worked, and where they had hoped that one day they would die. Illness and disability force many to leave familiar surroundings and their friends. The necessity of a new environment—a health care facility, group home, or hospital—often with its sterile four walls, bed, nightstand and chair, only seems to add to the confusion that has come to pervade their days and nights. Faces change every eight hours. Food is often bland. Stability, familiarity, and the smallest sense of security have disappeared. Like refugees in a strange land, these patients live each day with only their memories of what life used to be.

People like Sarah need us—you and me. They find happiness in those occasional visitors who have the patience and willingness to listen to an elderly woman describe her life on a farm in rural Maryland in the 1920s. From time to time we might have to listen to this story several times and endure the repetitive details of a life.

What people at end of life need more than any material comfort, is another human being who can offer an hour of their physical presence, to simply listen and be. Elizabeth Kubler-Ross reminds us in her book, *Life Lessons* that life does not end with the diagnosis of a life-challenging illness. This is when it truly begins. "It begins at this point because when you acknowledge the reality of your death, you also have to acknowledge the meaning of your life." Sarah knew she was approaching the end of her journey. She was not afraid of death. But she did want to tell her story, to share with others her true self.

The peace of mind we support in people's living into dying can be the greatest gift we offer. When the end approaches, many of us simply want peace. To us at hospice, the peace Sarah found in a simple visit from some one who would just listen, demonstrates the peace that many yearn for deep within. In her world, peace took on new meaning every day. Sometimes it was a cup of coffee served piping hot, whereas other days it was reassurance that the baby elephant outside her window would not be left an orphan. Peace was all that a 92-year-old woman wanted.

All of us tried to provide her with this same peace, and this was the goal for the hospice team. On that gray and cold December morning when we admitted Sarah to hospice, we saw the Divine image, but it had become clouded and dimmed by years of loneliness and abandonment. Now, with the help of so many fellow human beings who heard her silent plea and took action, the Divine image shone brighter and with greater resilience simply because we took the time to care. This is what all of us need to do. We are all Jesus.

The General

"Old soldiers never die. They just fade away."

General Douglas MacArthur

"Good morning General Smith." I greeted the general as usual, and as usual, there was no audible reply. Bowed over with his chin resting on his chest, he slowly lifted his head. He strained to open his eyes, and when he finally saw who had spoken to him, he looked intently at me. Perhaps he recognized me. I really could not tell. I had been visiting this patient for nearly nine months. Each time I visited, he appeared to be resting comfortably in his wheelchair at the nurses' station. General Smith had been a longtime resident of this facility, having struggled with Alzheimer's disease and dementia.

Alzheimer's disease is a dreadful wasting away of the mind and virtually all memory. Currently, there is no cure for the disease. Researchers have no clear indicators that a person is more or less likely to get the disease. One of the greatest challenges facing the medical community is the problem of the very fine line between normal memory loss and forgetfulness and the onset of Alzheimer's.

From a clinical standpoint, the disease is divided into three stages. At the onset, a person begins to forget little things. Keys are misplaced. Appointments are forgotten. The person maintains normal body function and manages normal daily activity and needs. As the disease progresses to the moderate stage, a person begins to forget the way home, or might be unable to recognize a family member or friend. There is loss of the capability of caring for oneself, needing assistance with daily life including bathing, cooking, and cleaning.

The disease makes fast gains over the mind. Soon a patient cannot recognize a spouse or how to avoid danger. Each day, the disease robs its victim of a life of memories. In the final stage, all higher brain function is lost. In most cases, the patient is in a vegetative state. Family and friends must provide complete care. They must feed, bathe, and dress their loved one.

A caregiver must readjust every day to the new loss of memory. This causes great stress and strain on the patient's caregiver, family, and friends. No sooner than the adjustment is made, then the loved one suffering from Alzheimer's succumbs to further memory loss, becoming increasingly dependent on those who provide care. Those things we once took for granted, are now daily burdens both physically and mentally. Many caregivers are beset with feelings of guilt, frustration, anger and a sense of hopelessness.

Yet, we must remember that a person in the throes of Alzheimer's is still a person. It is a disease of the mind, not the heart. It robs the patient of his or her humanity. Memories, relationships, and a sense of identity slowly fade. For those family and friends providing the 24-hour care, the process worsens as they watch a loved one disappear before their very eyes. At times, we only see the shell of the patient, who still needs to feel loved in ways that may not be easily achieved. Dignity, respect, courage and love are the essentials when caring for someone with Alzheimer's disease.

At this point in his life, the General faced his greatest battle, the daily fight against an unseen enemy slowly robbing him of his identity. This retired Marine Corps General, who had fought in many battles of the Pacific theater of operations during World War II, continued to stare at me wondering, I hoped, where he had heard that voice and seen that face in the past. Any visitor to this facility could see the devastation and debilitation of Alzheimer's disease, especially on this frail, hunched-over, retired general.

Nevertheless, I considered each visit an opportunity to break through this terrible disease and make some contact with my friend. Seated next to him in his wheelchair, I regarded this 88-year-old veteran with awe and reverence. I tried to imagine a young, spry, 25-year-old Marine officer trudging through the jungles of Guam, the Philippines, and countless other islands as bullets and rocket shells hurled past him and his comrades. Like so many of his generation, he made a great sacrifice. He fought a war against untold aggression where millions of innocent men, women, and children had died. If left unchecked, these aggressors would have continued their brutal attacks on civilians until they had achieved their goal of global domination. The general was willing to put his life on the line so that future generations might live in peace.

During our visits, I would ask him questions about the war and about his experiences on the battlefield. "General, did you ever get hit by enemy fire? How many of your buddies got hit? Did you ever have doubts about making it home alive? How did your faith in God help you?" With each question, I paused hoping for an answer or a nod or any other indication that my voice was penetrating beyond the grip of a disease that seemed as impregnable as the enemy machine-gunner nests did more than half a century ago. But, each question and each hope-filled pause was met with no reply. The general was deep in thought somewhere, but not with me.

∞

This is precisely the point when a family member, loved one, or caregiver might give up any hope of communicating with an Alzheimer's patient. Countless hours are spent with people who have the disease. Those who care for loved ones with this disease often describe their efforts as meaningless. The constant repetition of a question or endless hours of blank stares can push any one to the brink. No matter what we may try, nothing seems to work.

As the days turn into weeks, months, and years, we may grow bitter and even resentful. This is when we need to persist with our efforts to communicate with a loved who is suffering from this illness. We need to remind ourselves that there is someone present among us. They hear. They see. They feel. Alzheimer's disease attacks the mind, but not the heart. Scripture gives us hope, "For where your treasure its, there your heart will be also." (Lk 12:34)

Although perhaps physically unable to tell us what we want to hear, they are ever present among us. We ought to demonstrate great compassion and care with our words and our actions just as we did with them prior to their illness. I recall my family's 18-month journey of care with my grandmother. Mom, along with her three sisters, provided round-the-clock care for their 92-year-old mother who was suffering from dementia. One day, my grandmother turned to my mom and said, "I'm glad you girls don't argue over me." These were the first words she had spoken in days. They brought joy and hope to a situation that seemed without joy and hopeless. The story also reinforces how and why we need to treat those with Alzheimer's and dementia with love and respect.

Our persistence must be carried out lovingly and with patience. Hebrew scripture reminds us all to be patient. "I waited on the Lord, and He heard my cry." (Ps 40:1).

I often spoke with nursing-home staff about their feelings toward the General and other Alzheimer patients. With most, the main concern was their level of patience with the patient. My recommendation was always the same, "persistence and patience." These are the two keys to successfully treating our loved ones who suffer from Alzheimer's disease.

When a tragedy like Alzheimer's disease strikes, we may blame an angry God or the victim. But God has not turned his back on us, nor has the person earned such a punishment. Rather, we must learn to accept pain and suffering in our lives. As we come to terms with our mortality, we need to learn and demonstrate patience and persistence. Alzheimer's disease is the enemy, not the loved one who is desperately trying to break free from its grip. Remember, the disease destroys the mind, not the heart. Our efforts are always appreciated whether or not the patient can express appreciation. Our patience and persistence determines the quality of care for those suffering from the disease.

∞

On one unusually rainy morning, while I was visiting hospice patients at this same facility, I spotted the General. As usual, he was sitting in his wheelchair, head slumped forward, chin resting on his chest, and deep in thought. I crouched down beside him and announced my arrival. "Good morning, General. It's Matthew the hospice chaplain. How are you feeling today?"

There was no verbal response, even though I knew somewhere deep inside he, like other victims of Alzheimer's disease, gained some hope from this sort of dialogue. Although physically unable to acknowledge my presence, at a spiritual level, he knew some one was taking time to speak to him, to affirm that he was still a human being. His life had meaning. So I waited, trying to think of something clever, something to bring him back from the distant voyage this disease often imposes upon its unfortunate passengers.

"Hey General, did you ever see a chaplain with a pony tail like mine? I'm sure you don't have many of them in the Marine Corps!"

The words of that last sentence must have opened a small window into the world of General Smith. He lifted his head with the same deliberate and slow motion he had made on previous visits. His eyes opened, revealing the deep blue color his medical chart described, which few had seen since the disease had progressed to its advanced stage.

He stared at me intently, and I smiled as he continued to look at me—this chaplain with long hair. I looked into his eyes expecting to find some truth, some information or some indication he knew I was with him. I hoped he would look into my eyes and see that I was his friend, someone who cared, someone who understood his struggle. We are taught to look someone straight in the eyes to see if they are honest, sincere, and trustworthy. Eyes can tell us a lot about a person; I was hoping he would be able to see me for who I was.

The blue in his eyes seemed to come alive with a vibrancy and clarity I had not seen during my previous visits. Perhaps the General had been able to fight his way back to his old self before the disease could rob him of any normal means of communication. At that moment, he seemed to have escaped the grip of his disease. So I decided to ask him another question. "Would you like me to say a prayer?"

The words seemed to travel forever as his facial expression changed from pleasantly confused to somewhat familiar. After a few moments, which seemed to me like several long minutes, I heard a faint, but definite voice reply, "Yeah, but make it a short one." I remained there, crouched by his side, waiting for more of what I had hoped for since beginning to visit the General nearly nine months earlier.

He spoke no more but wore an expression on his face that indicated he was patiently waiting for my prayer, my short prayer.

We prayed, and when I had finished, he looked me straight in the eye for a moment, then slowly closed his eyes, bowing his head to its usual position with his chin resting on his chest. My window into his world had opened briefly, enabling me to communicate with the real General Smith. His one sentence, "Yeah, but make it a short one," was the only time he spoke to me during my visits with him. Yet, it remains one of the brightest moments in my ministry at hospice and a great victory for me in the constant and often frustrating struggle with Alzheimer's disease.

Our loved ones saddled with Alzheimer dementia are still people. They are human beings capable of experiencing love, fear, pain, sorrow, and the joys of human interaction. Often, we perceive their inability to communicate as an unwillingness to acknowledge our presence; we view their behavior as aggressive or combative. In reality, a person in the grips of Alzheimer's and dementia are trying just as hard to break free of its hold as we are trying to communicate with them.

Our attitude toward them needs to be one of care, compassion, and unconditional love. We must continue to converse with them, lovingly embrace them, and let them know they still matter to us. Our presence with them is essential, and we need to direct our efforts to be fully present with them on a regular basis. The disease is not easy; no one should feel guilty about placing a loved one with Alzheimer's into an assisted-living facility or nursing home. No one, no matter how superhuman they may think they are, can do it alone. We all need help, and there are many facilities out there that can offer the help we need.

Being Honest With Buddy

"When you acknowledge the reality of death, you
also acknowledge the meaning of life."
Elizabeth Kubler-Ross

"When he dies, I am going to kill myself." Nadine frantically replied as she choked back the tears, taking another tissue from her purse wiping away the stream of tears which had trickled down her exceptionally youthful face. Her words forced the social worker and me to readjust ourselves and take serious note. When health-care professionals sense any sign or hear any mention of suicide, we immediately document the event and inform the hospice-care team of the level of concern. In this instance, Nadine may or may not have been serious, but we had to be ready.

She and Buddy had been married for 35 years. He was her knight in shining armor, having rescued her from an abusive father at the early age of 17. She had placed her trust, her very existence, into Buddy's gentle and loving care. Although he was 16 years older than she when they decided to make a life together, after dating for several years, the age difference was never a consideration. She was a stunning woman at 56, while he looked the part of an older man, but certainly not someone in his early 70s and facing an end-of-life illness.

Nadine dug deep into her purse searching for another tissue. The tears continued to roll down her cheeks eventually set-
tling onto her lap. Her emotional display expressed a genuine
love, a truly caring, terribly confused wife, desperately seeking
answers to a problem with only one certain outcome: She was
losing Buddy. He was dying, and neither she nor any one else
could stop it.

∞

Whether we take time to realize it or not, we eventually lose
everything we possess or have accumulated over a lifetime, except
for those things that truly matter. Houses, cars, jobs, investments,
and other material items are merely on loan. Family and friends
relocate and move away. In the end, death takes those we love
most, those with whom we have established relationships, with
whom we have built our lives. These tangible, items as well as
our dreams, our hopes, even our independence, will one day
come to an end.

From a theological standpoint, all that we possess or acquire
is not ours, but rather a gift. "Every good gift, every perfect
gift is from above, and comes down from the Father of lights."
(Jas 1:17)

The accumulation of wealth, power, friendships, and even
our health is temporary. We are not possessors, but merely stewards granted these gifts for a brief period of time. Those who
try to find permanence in these worldly things often fail. Those
who spend great effort to prevent the inevitable loss ultimately
arrive at disillusionment with all.

What matters most in life, the one possession that death can
never take from us, is love. Love is the one aspect of life which
endures beyond any physical, emotional, or spiritual loss. With
love, hope exists, dreams continue; lives are lived to their fullest,

most sincere and honest authenticity. Love never fails, even when death takes a loved one from our midst. The love remains, being a source of comfort if we accept our mortality as a normal event in our lives. We need to confront our fear of death and loss with honesty and sincerity.

The inevitable loss each of us will face does not need to be a source of sadness or hopelessness in our lives. On the contrary, a healthy realization of the truth can give us a deeper appreciation for the beauty and wonder, the fruits of an honest and open life. Many of us speak of life as a school, the lessons we learn being the experiences we gain from living life; loss is a major part of our coursework. In our loss, we come face to face with who we are and with what matters most. We may experience unconditional love from our spouse, family, friends, and even total strangers providing care or comfort for us in our time of need. Most often, we recognize this love as end of life approaches.

The noted physician and author Dr. Bernie Siegel reminds his patients and readers that "awareness of our mortality is a gift that enables us to live better." At first, Dr. Siegel's words may seem paradoxical, but they emphasize the simple fact our mortality, our inevitable death, is not to be feared, but embraced when that time comes. Death is not the problem even though it might frighten us. It is our feelings and misconceptions about death that pose the greatest stumbling blocks as we face end of life. The sooner we accept that one day we will die, the sooner we will alter the way we live our life. If we gave thought to our mortality each day, we might change the way we view our life, and begin to live life more authentically, honestly, and lovingly, rather than with regret, reluctance, and missed opportunities.

As a hospice chaplain, I've seen and heard how patients and their families deal with the discovery that death is approaching.

When the physician tells them that the illness is terminal and medical science can no longer help them, some desperately seek any means of obtaining a second chance on life. Promises are made. Oaths are taken. Both patient and family seek some way of escape from this horrible fate. Prior to the terminal diagnosis, they may have spent very little time contemplating the attitudes and actions of their daily lives. Unaware of their influence upon others, some may have been living without a spiritual barometer, an internal guidance system, the little voice that speaks from the heart, to constantly remind them to keep striving for ways of loving themselves and those around them.

Having learned of their terminal illness, they want to seize all missed opportunities, reliving moments of regret and poor judgment. They want to perform in a manner that would benefit not only themselves, but those around them. When we come to realize our own mortality, we truly live life in its authenticity. The sooner we understand that death is inevitable and begin to live in the present, we can begin to live more fully without regret, remorse, or fear. Few of us ever receive a second chance. Each of us needs to "live each day as if it were the last."

∞

Nadine resumed her conversation with us, "Do you know how good this man is?" She asked us as if she were about to deliver a tribute; to an ordinary, yet heroic man who had always been there for her. When hospice professionals encounter such remarkable patients and their families, we, too, experience a profound rush of emotion. Our eyes also well up with tears as husbands, wives, children, and friends describe in great detail the words and deeds of a loved one facing end of life. At times, we want to take up the banner and join them in their praise of a loved one facing death, of someone we may have just met.

Like so many of us, Nadine was afraid of death. Here was a good man, a kind man, a loving man, in her words the "perfect husband." He now faced the final weeks of his existence. The fear of loss seemed overwhelming, and this fear is quite common. Each of us has a fear that haunts our lives. For some of us, it is speaking in public, while loneliness or even driving a car frightens others. Dealing with our fears can be a difficult task. How can we live with our fears?

∞

Fear is multi-layered and must be addressed layer by layer. Love, along with honesty and sincerity, are the only defense against fear. If we fail to overcome our fears, our relationship with ourselves and with those around us will begin to suffer. Fear is a dangerous beast that gives birth to anger, resentment, guilt, and even hatred. These ills work against us and our loved ones. Approaching the core of fear, one often finds the fear of death as the root of all the others. This fear causes us to turn from our authentic selves in search of inadequacies. "I'm not good enough, smart enough, pretty enough, tall enough, brave enough, etc." Meanwhile doubt creeps into our life as we decide that others are all those things and more. We retreat from our true selves and hide within the many layers of fear and condemnation.

With this attitude we unknowingly harm ourselves and our loved ones. Fear drives us to hold back our true thoughts, our true feelings, and our true words. As the fear gains possession of us, we hold ourselves back personally and professionally, stifling our authentic self. We are no longer honest with ourselves or with our loved ones. As the fear grows, relationships suffer, families drift apart, and loneliness, isolation, and even depression set in.

Facing a terminal illness, it is ironic that dying makes our worst fears come to life. Dying forces us to face them honestly, authentically, and completely. Dying helps us to live more fully in the present, to confront fears which have kept us prisoners shackled in chains and irons of our own making throughout a lifetime. We can shed our fears and try to live the rest of life to its fullest.

To transcend fear, we must leap into the realm of love. Where there is love, there can be no fear. Where fear is, there also is the absence of love. From love flows happiness, joy, and peace. In his Epistle, St. John, the Disciple whom Jesus called "the beloved" writes, "Perfect love casts out fear." (1 Jn 4:18) There is no time or place that love and fear can coexist. Throughout our lives each moment offers an opportunity to choose between the two. This is especially true when end-of-life approaches and the fear of loss challenges our commitment to choose love. Love nourishes the soul, strengthens the body, and reinvigorates the mind, uniting all three on a level that drives fear away.

∞

Nadine and Buddy shared a life of love. They lived authentically, honestly, and sincerely throughout their 35 years together. Nadine had fought many battles with fear, struggling through each layer on her own and with the help of her loving companion by her side. Now, facing the greatest fear of all, the loss of her most precious possession, Buddy, death seemed an insurmountable foe. She grasped for clues or insights into battle with this greatest of fears.

We continued our conversation with Nadine, allowing her time to gather her thoughts and voice her concerns, whatever they might be. She seemed a bit calmer, somewhat relieved that she could confide in us and share her fear of death. Above all, she needed someone who would listen, and so we did just that. Nadine began with a story from their early years of marriage, delving into her husband's gentle manner toward her and the children. "He never raised a hand against me or the children. Yet, if someone wanted to fight, he could hold his own, and that man never picked another fight with my Buddy again." A smile returned to her face, and she laughed as she described some funnier incidents where Buddy displayed both brains and brawn. As she continued to relive and retell her life with her beloved husband, we, the hospice team at her side, breathed a sigh of relief gaining confidence that Nadine was not going to kill herself, not yet, and hopefully not ever.

Although overcome with grief and deep anguish with the recent diagnosis of her husband's terminal illness, and responding to this news in an extreme manner by mentioning the possibility of suicide, Nadine's initial question to us concerning the goodness of her husband was an unconscious start with coming to terms with end of life. For most of her married life, she had spent little time thinking about death or the inevitable separation that would occur when she or Buddy died. Now, she was facing end-of-life issues and struggling with her first bout of grief, a form known as anticipatory grief. She knew he was dying but did not know when. What she needed now was a chance to process the grief, to tell the story of a life of love, a life lived authentically. Nadine was about to begin her first of many life-review stories, ones that would guide her feelings and emotions toward accepting the terminal diagnosis. Her acceptance would serve as a vehicle for expressing grief and loss, and allow her to journey with Buddy preparing for the death that would indeed separate them in this earthly life.

Nadine is like so many of our patients' spouses. The numbing chill that overwhelms loved ones when they hear their doctor's words that the patient has only a few weeks or months to live, or even a few days, hits them like a punch to the stomach.

These words from a medical doctor leave us breathless, empty, completely at a loss. Words fail to accurately describe the immediate loss combined with the torrential crush of grief that descends upon loved ones, especially when the doctor follows up such devastating news with, "Would you like to have hospice involved with the care of your loved one?" By this point in the conversation, those who had been able to hold things together, who had managed to gain some control over their emotions, now openly sob and shake their heads with utter disbelief.

This is where Nadine was with us on that afternoon in the nursing home. She managed to find some balance between tacit acceptance and complete despair. Her faith in God, her faith in the medical profession, and her faith in herself hung in the balance. One wrong word on our part, one hesitation or sign of uncertainty might translate in her mind as a situation of complete hopelessness. Suicide would not just be an option; it would be her answer. She would go just as he slipped from this world, just as his heart beat for its final time. This would be her signal. This would be her permission slip to commit the unthinkable—taking her life.

Nadine recognized that she could do nothing to stop the illness from taking the most important thing in her life, her husband. But she would soon discover over the next three months the unexpected reward in acceptance; acceptance of the fact that death comes to all of us one day. She would learn to face it head on, without denying its place in the very fabric of life. Honesty in all matters would be her road to the acceptance of this impending loss. It would be a rough road, yet one she would travel with courage, accompanied by family and friends; a road sprinkled with both uncertainty and unexpected episodes of laughter and joy along the way.

By the end of our first meeting, she reluctantly agreed to have hospice assist in the care of her beloved Buddy on one condition: he was not to know that he was dying. We were to enter the room, introduce ourselves by our name and position, and act as if we were part of the nursing home staff who would be visiting him on a regular basis. Nadine believed that her husband's illness, end-stage brain cancer, would take his life before he ever realized that he was a man in the final stages of his life.

It is my firm belief that a person needs to be told that they are seriously ill, and allow that patient to ask more questions regarding the illness. No patient should be told that he or she is dying. When patients are ready to face the issue of death and dying, we ought to listen to their concerns, their questions, and then answer them honestly. No one, not doctors, not social workers, not even chaplains, should ever play God, who alone knows the certain truth, and tell someone that he or she is going to die. Patients need not be forced to face their own death when they are unprepared to do so. The family, together with the physician, social worker, and chaplain, can work out a way to present the information when the patient requests answers to difficult questions.

We agreed to her request even though we had some reservations. Honesty is clearly what we seek in all parts of the hospice plan of care, but we must respect the wishes of our families. The hospice team wanted Nadine to tell Buddy that he was very sick, to plant a seed that might prompt Buddy to ask some important questions about the illness and end of life. People facing end of life need to prepare. They have a lot of work to accomplish in a very small amount of time. We tried several ways to convince Nadine to share some news with her husband. With tears still flowing down her cheeks, she replied, "I just can't do that to him."

In the end, we agreed to her terms. It was the only way she could continue, to move forward and tread slowly into the realm of facing her loss, as the death of Buddy grew closer every day. As we all expected, Buddy warmly received all of our team members' visits, including mine. Although tired and somewhat confused because of the illness, he spoke clearly and firmly when he was at his best. He seemed especially ready to talk about the things he enjoyed most in his life, the love he had for his wife and family, and the comfort he received from prayer. In my mind, Buddy, like Nadine, was also engaged in life review, the first stage in preparing for an eventual death.

On occasion he would ask how things were going at my parish. When I spoke to him that attendance could be better, he replied with a sly grin, "Don't worry, Chaplain, they'll be by when they hear how good you preach." His concern and encouragement were genuine, as he would remind me that when he got his strength back, he'd come by and help with the building project that our parish was planning. Throughout our visits, the topic of death, end of life and hospice were never mentioned.

Nonetheless, I sensed a tangible, but unspoken, understanding on Buddy's part that something was terribly wrong with his health. In some sense, he knew he was dying. He recognized that he was not always himself, and the daily visits by his brother, his daughters and his wife, along with distant relatives and friends, only reinforced his unspoken intuition. Deep down, he knew, but possibly did not want to burden his wife with another matter of concern. He never asked any of us to discuss end of life or to prepare his wife for the final days that remained.

This approach of dealing with hospice bothered me. I realized it was the family's wish that Buddy not know about his terminal diagnosis. Yet, I often think how we entertain the same approach in crisis situations throughout our life when fear gains control over reason, forcing us to stray from our authentic self unable to recognize who we are.

∞

I remember as a young child an incident in which I was cutting cardboard with a sharp utility knife. As I bore down on the blade to ensure a clean and deep cut, I placed my left hand along the straightedge to provide added stability. With a good amount of pressure, I began to draw the knife along the straightedge. Without warning, the blade snapped, and I drove the remaining portion of the blade into my left index finger.

Immediately, the blood flowed from the cut, and I hurried off to the bathroom where I washed the wound and gathered the necessary ointment and bandages. My mother knocked at the door and asked if everything was all right. She knew something had happened; she sensed the crisis at hand. Naturally, I replied that there was nothing wrong, and waited for her to leave before I removed my hand from under the towel and finished my first-aid care.

When I emerged from the bathroom, my mother asked me to come to the kitchen. As I approached the doorway, she politely asked, "So how deep is the wound?" Although I wanted to deny any harm, to raise my hand and say, "See, no cuts," I couldn't. I broke down in tears and ran to her for comfort and support. I had tried to conceal the truth out of fear of what others might think.

Those we love, with whom we develop a relationship built on love and trust, know us. They develop a bond with us that bind together our energies—we are truly soul mates. When something unforeseen occurs, a signal is transmitted by our actions or by a change in our tone of voice. My mother knew immediately that something was wrong, but gave me the chance to acknowledge my mistake and share the truth. I might not have had the emotional breakdown if I had told her the truth and allowed her to share in my pain and ease my moment of crisis. But I feared what might happen if I told the truth. I made the choice to conceal reality, to drown out what my heart was saying and play along with the silly game of ego.

∞

This story illustrates to some extent how Nadine and Buddy dealt with his terminal illness. Since neither of them had agreed to be honest with each other about the end-of-life crisis facing them, no one could yet begin to enjoy the benefits of the healing process that comes with being honest when facing any impending crisis. His death was literally a time bomb in their lives. Although it would go off, they clung to a possibility that the explosion could be muted, that the blast could be lessened so as to be barely audible. Both of them knew he was dying, and both of them were too frightened to acknowledge this reality. Both of them resisted facing their greatest fear, the fear of death, and so they lost some valuable time that could have been spent on healing and bringing hope even in the face of a terminal illness.

All of this changed on one quiet Sunday afternoon. Nadine arrived at the nursing home on a particularly sunny morning. She had driven the route so often that she joked about driving to the nursing home in her sleep. As she passed by the nurses' station on her way to Buddy's room, she smiled and greeted the nurses with a cheery, "Good morning. Everything quiet so far?"

The nurses, sitting at their station and filling out the endless pages of paperwork which consumes more and more of their day, looked up and greeted Nadine with the same familiar tone of voice, "Hey there, beautiful. It's real quiet right now. How are you doing? And why aren't you home getting a little rest on such a beautiful morning?" The nurse's question was more of a statement than a real inquiry. They knew that she visited every day, and arrived early on Sunday.

Nadine paused and said, "I am pooped, but he is my greatest love in the world, and I knew he'd do the same for me if we were in opposite places." The nurses simply smiled and nodded. Many of the residents endured days and sometimes weeks without a visitor. For some, the staff of the facility were the only ones who tried to spend some time with those who had no one to stop in and hold a hand or sit quietly for a few minutes. "No one should be alone, Chaplain," said a nurse with whom I had become friends since my first visit to the nursing home as hospice chaplain. "How true," I replied knowing how nurses struggled to spend time with their patients, especially those who had little or no family.

Buddy's voice greeted Nadine as she entered his room. "Hey good looking, get over here and give me a kiss." She smiled, and gave him a tender, loving kiss. He looked exceptionally good that morning. He had been given a shower and shave just before she arrived. He was wearing a new pair of pajamas that made him look better than he felt. The cancer was spreading; he had been steadily losing weight. He realized his final days were approaching. He wanted to clear up some issues. Looking at his wife, he told her to sit by his side. He took her hand, and squeezed it once, as couples do when they want to say things are going to be okay when they are not.

With little warning, Buddy looked at his wife and said, "You know, I need to pick out a suit for my funeral."

Nadine heard the words, but could not believe what she had just heard. She stared at him without saying a word. She was in shock. A series of questions raced through her mind: how does he know that he is dying; who told him; why was he told this news without permission. As the questions continued to crowd her mind, Buddy interrupted.

"I know that I am dying, and I've known it for a while now. No one told me. I just felt it inside me. I see it on your face and the kids' faces. Hell, even family I don't like visit me." He tried to get his wife to smile, but she couldn't. She continued to stare, only hearing a portion of what he was saying. Thoughts continued to crowd her mind. She desperately sought ways to change what she had just heard from her husband's own lips. Again, he interrupted her thoughts, "Hey, you listening to me? I need to pick out a suit for my funeral."

Nadine burst into tears and buried her face in her husband's chest. He rubbed her back without saying a word. She remained close to him for a long time. Then, she looked up into his face. The mascara and eyeliner had run down her face in long streaks of black and greenish blue. He smiled, and used his pajama sleeve to wipe away the smudges and said, "Hey, you going on the warpath or something?" She laughed a bit as more tears fell, kissing his face over and over leaving small blotches of black and greenish blue in a random pattern over his face saying, "Now both of us are on the warpath."

Fear, the fear of death, had held both Buddy and Nadine from living life to its fullest during those first weeks with hospice. Fear had robbed them of the honesty they had shared all of their life. Confronted by the loss of each other, both realized that love is all that matters. Overcoming fear, love regained its foothold in their life, allowing the return of an honest, authentic life. Instead of sidestepping their fear of dying, they could face it together and discover a greater meaning in things shared and in who they were. Love dispelled fear, allowing them to live in the present. They accepted the reality of the illness, and the rest of the family followed their example. When circumstances were at their worst, they discovered what was best. They listened to the inner voice of their hearts.

Most of us will find peace and contentment in life when we release the conditions we place on our love for each other. These conditions are shackles on our relationships. If we release them, we find love in many ways we never thought possible. Relationships offer us the biggest opportunities for learning in our journey of life. We discover who we are, what we fear, where our strengths come from and the meaning of true love: there are no mistakes in relationships. From the very first meeting with our loved one to the final adieu, we live a life of learning. Love shared frees us for honesty and authenticity, frees us to live life to its fullest, even when facing death.

The remaining weeks brought new insights into end of life for Buddy, Nadine, and their family. They grew to accept the impending death of their loved one without forsaking the opportunity for growth and love. One daughter, who had become estranged over the past years and rarely saw her father, began to visit regularly, keeping watch by her father's bedside as the final days approached. Only a few months ago, she would have never set foot in the same room with her father. Now she kept vigil, praying in silence for a peaceful, painless, end, with family by the bedside as her father's soul would eventually leave his body.

All of our fears involve either the past or the uncertainty of the future. Love lives in and for the present. Now, the present is all we have, and love is the most powerful emotion because it exists in the present. To live in the present is to live in love. That was the goal for Buddy and his family. That goal should be all of ours: to live in love, to live authentically, honestly, and in the present.

Gingerbread Lady

"You cannot discover new oceans unless you
lose sight of the shore."
Tibetan Proverb

Hospice provides care for a wide spectrum of people. We deal with patients and families who bring with them their entire lifetime of living. We learn about their strengths and their weaknesses, their achievements and their failures, their dreams fulfilled, and those that remain unresolved. As health-care providers working with people in the final days of their life on earth, we ought to come to them without any agenda offering them the best in end-of-life care.

Many patients come to us with histories of experience beyond imagination. While aiming for a patient and family to accept the reality of end of life, rarely does the hospice confront a set of beliefs that are contrary to hospice philosophy.

Pearl, whom *The Washington Post* dubbed, "Gingerbread Lady," was one of those extraordinary individuals. Married to a military career officer, she had traveled around the world, immersing herself and her family in many foreign cultures. While stationed in Germany following World War II, Pearl became fascinated by the custom of gingerbread baking at Christmas time. She enrolled in some baking courses and learned the specifics of gingerbread baking and making gingerbread houses.

Many Christmas seasons of gingerbread-house making later, the Smithsonian Institution invited her to bake a gingerbread house for the 1992 holiday season. It was a success. Each year for the next eight years, the Smithsonian would ask for a different gingerbread house, and each year Pearl would design, bake, and build a house as authentic in design as the model she had been assigned to make.

In 1999, the Smithsonian asked her to make a gingerbread house in the shape of the White House. Pearl gasped with disbelief at such a daunting task. This type of house posed several problems, including the most obvious one gingerbread is brown, not white, and the frosting is really a glue, not a good wall covering. But she created a model complete with wrought iron fencing (stick pretzels dipped in chocolate) and all 84 windows. The nation's premier museum was overwhelmed by her effort. Record crowds visited during the Christmas season, and everyone gazed at the unique replica of the nation's first home. Visitors stopped by and chatted with Pearl, who answered questions about her project; she even offered young visitors a chance to decorate their very own gingerbread cookies. She had baked over 1,500 of them for children to decorate while visiting the museum.

It was also during that Christmas season of 1999 that Pearl began to feel more tired. Everyday activities became a burden. She went to the doctors. Tests revealed that the cancer diagnosed four years earlier had begun to spread. She had beaten the odds thus far, but she knew her body was tiring. When she finally came to hospice, she was at peace with her diagnosis and her terminal illness. She had battled cancer for nearly six years. Pearl was not one to sugar coat her life.

The morning of our first meeting was a surprise. Pearl lived in a retirement facility for military officers and their spouses. She also worked in the "Treasure Chest," a store which sold bric-a-brac, housedresses, and other items donated by residents and their families. In some ways, it was an upscale thrift store, and I often visited the shop to purchase an inexpensive gift for a patient's birthday. Pearl had volunteered many hours at the shop, and remembered me. "I am glad that you are finally here."

My mind began to delve deep into its hospice folders wondering if she had some deep religious issue or end-of-life philosophical question that needed to be answered. I stood at that door as she reached into her sweater pocket and pulled out a quarter. As she placed it into my hand, she sighed deeply and said, "A few weeks ago you came into the Thrift Shop and purchased some item. I cheated you out of a quarter's change. There we're even now." I smiled and thanked her realizing that this was her burning issue of the moment. She turned, walked back to her chair, and sat down. That initial greeting was brief, but a start.

After some general conversation and a short video clip from the local Washington TV station that featured her and the Gingerbread White House she had created in 1999, we discussed matters pertaining to end of life and her diagnosis. She was at peace on all levels. I asked, as I do with all hospice patients that I visit, whether or not she would like to close with a prayer. She replied, in almost a shy way, "You might not want to pray with me when I tell you how I feel."

For a moment I wondered with some concern, what I might have said in the previous hour that might have created any discomfort. Was there a word or phrase that could have expressed any bias on my part? Was I not a good listener, giving her time to tell me her story? What could possibly have happened during this initial meeting that might jeopardize any future visits?

As the last thought crossed my mind, Pearl resumed her explanation. "I am a Christian and have been all my life. As a child, my mother took me to church every Sunday. My husband and I were married at a military chapel, and we attended services wherever we were stationed. But some of my personal beliefs may make you feel uncomfortable." She paused and looked at me with an intent seriousness followed by a sigh.

Again, my mind raced with possible scenarios, but this process was interrupted by her voice as she spoke. "I believe in God, and in the Bible, but I also believe in reincarnation. I know this goes against all of Christian teaching, but over the years I have read a lot on the subject, and have experienced some things that lead me to believe that I have lived several lives before this one and will live several more after I depart this one. You, as a minister, may not like this, so I wanted to tell you up front. If you don't feel comfortable with my beliefs, then I won't be offended if you choose not to visit me again."

Silence filled the room. She seemed at peace with her declaration of faith, and the tension which filled the room just a few minutes ago had vanished. I took both of her hands into mine and expressed my gratitude for her honesty and openness. Without speaking a word, the action of my hands gently holding hers demonstrated my respect for her beliefs no matter how they might differ from mine or for that matter the teachings of the faith.

Often, at the end of life, our patients and their families search for words they think we (hospice professionals) want to hear. They are frightened, uncertain of the journey that they are about to embark upon, and do not wish to alienate anyone along the journey. Nonetheless, our patients and their families need guides, fellow travelers along this part of the journey. A terminal illness creates fear and pain in the uncertain future awaiting everyone involved. It can open up old wounds buried deep within the folds of the fabric of our lives. As Pearl, the

Gingerbread Lady, spoke from her heart, a sense of peace filled the small apartment.

Her firm clasp on my hands expressed her gratitude for my acceptance of her beliefs without passing judgment. "Thank you. Thank you for your honesty." I spoke with a slight hint of relief in my voice. "I would love to visit you as often as you wish."

She smiled. "That would be fine. You can put me on the list of regular visits when you make your rounds at this facility."

"Now before I leave, I need to ask you something that I ask all the people I visit when we conclude our time together. Would you like to close with a prayer?" Without any hesitations she responded, "A prayer would be a fine thing." So we prayed and continued to pray for guidance, mercy, and peace each time I visited.

Her beliefs had made me step back in my role as hospice chaplain and examine just what my calling might ask of me. I must admit that I did find it a bit unusual for an elderly woman, whom many referred to as "Gingerbread Lady" to profess a belief in reincarnation. If she had been from a country where tradition had taught this belief, it might have been less of a surprise. But she was born and raised in a Christian household in Oregon. The Gingerbread Lady's honesty made me readjust my own definition of what it was that I do.

Earlier, I defined spirituality in the hospice setting as offering presence and purpose. This definition encompasses a "being" aspect and a "doing" aspect. These are not separate entities, but combine to bring healing as a loved one faces the end of their earthly life. The chaplain needs to consider many factors in the realm of spiritual care, and often experiences many surprises. My greatest challenge yet was this sweet, elderly woman's belief in reincarnation.

Sitting in the quiet of my house chapel, I reflected on my visit with the Gingerbread Lady. What were the most important things in my life? I listed the following: my faith, my family, my parishioners, the hospice staff and our patients, those suffering in body and soul, and my garden. If I were facing a terminal illness, I would want these same aspects considered. I realized that I would need those around me to accept me and my beliefs. Above all I hoped that those providing my care would be respectful of my wishes.

∞

The desire to have others respect our wishes and our directives is one of the greatest concerns that will arise in us as we enter into the final stages of our lives. Autonomy, the independence we enjoy in making our every decision in our life, slowly erodes as a disease progresses. Regardless of age, income, or social status, if we are in the midst of a terminal illness, we become more dependent upon others for the fulfillment of needs.

Initially, we may ask others for help with household chores, meal preparation, and some personal care. As an illness progresses, we lose more of our autonomy in all areas of our life. Finally we become dependent upon others for our every care and comfort. Both body and soul come to rely upon others to help guide us along our journey. In the spiritual realm of care, hospice chaplains can offer a great deal of comfort. As health-care professionals, we derive our knowledge and experience from a body of teaching covering in depth the value and needs of every aspect of life.

For most chaplains, this body of teaching is the Judeo-Christian tradition. Within this tradition, chaplains study theological and philosophical teachings which serve as a framework to all aspects of humanity. The Judeo-Christian tradition defines each of us as individuals who seek a belief in, or sense of belonging to, a religious tradition or spiritual practice. Each person in society seeks a meaning to life, and some set of guidelines by which this meaning can be realized. For many, these guidelines include love for family, love for humanity, love for nature, a desire for peace, autonomy, respect, honesty, and dignity.

When we enter into the final days of our journey on earth, the need to find meaning in life does not end. On the contrary, it is precisely at this time when finding some meaning in life takes on the greatest importance. Each of us needs to know that our wishes and desires will be respected. This includes our beliefs about life and the life to come.

∞

As I sat in the quiet of the chapel, I realized that the Gingerbread Lady had been placed in my life for a reason. She was not going to change my beliefs nor ask me to change hers. She merely wanted someone to listen to her story. She wanted to find meaning as she entered into the final days of her journey. She was searching for a peaceful journey, and I was one person who could be a companion and guide along the way. She had accepted me for who I was without any explanation or restrictions. The least I could do would be to accept her for who she was.

When we are true to ourselves, we learn to live life to its fullest. With peace of mind, we can express all of our feelings whether they be anger, anxiety, depression or happiness, joy, and love. Our feelings are unhealthy only if they remain buried, deep inside, and avoided. Letting people know who we are and where we are in life gives us and others a clear picture of who we are. There are fewer hidden surprises or disappointments if we deal honestly with our thoughts and beliefs. This brings greater peace and allows us to make progress in the final days of our journey on this earth.

The Gingerbread Lady was not trying to test me. She did not want to get some reaction or feel superior in any way. She was simply being honest to herself and honest with me. Letting me know who she was, what she thought, and what she believed. She placed no restrictions on me, nor did she ask me to believe or think like her. All she asked was that I accept her for who she was—an elderly woman waiting to embark on her new and uncharted journey.

Letter Board

"Unfinished business isn't about death. It's about life."
Elisabeth Kubler-Ross

A	E	I	O	U/Y
B	C	D	F	G
H	J	K	L	M
N	P	Q	R	S
T	V	W	X	Z

Since I was a young boy, I have enjoyed listening to a group of people engaged in simple conversation or deeply entrenched in a debate of some importance. Often, while my friends or cousins were out playing or participating in other childhood activities, I would seat myself amidst the company of older neighbors and relatives and listen intently to their topic of conversation.

The ability to engage in conversation and to actively listen to others is an important quality of the hospice chaplain. When a chaplain enters a private home or nursing facility, those first words and actions often set the tone for a particular visit, especially if it is the initial one. Patients and their families need someone who truly cares. They look for signs of an individual who will listen faithfully and quietly while they explain their thoughts and feelings.

These moments of "silently being present" offer the chaplain an opportunity to search the spiritual landscape of patients and their loved ones. Like a physician or nurse who listens to a patient's heart or lungs during a preliminary diagnosis, the chaplain approaches in a similar fashion during a visit with patients and their loved ones. In some cases, a few words may indicate a spiritual concern awaiting some clarification or explanation. It might open an avenue for discussion in the realm of spiritual care, not only for the patient and family, but also for others associated with the end-of-life event, including the hospice staff.

Communication is the key to a peaceful journey for all of hospice. The patient, family, and hospice staff need honest and open lines of communication to ensure proper care. With some patients an illness makes it virtually impossible to communicate in any conventional way and other methods must be employed in order to understand their needs and concerns. I soon discovered how an illness can challenge understanding and communication during my initial visit with Helen, a 47-year-old woman suffering from Progressive Pseudo Bulbar Palsy.

This disease is devastating. It slowly attacks and destroys motor nerves in the spinal cord and brain leading to progressive muscle weakness and eventual paralysis. There is no effective treatment or cure. Like all motor neuron disorders, such as Amyotrophic Lateral Sclerosis (Lou Gehrig's disease), Progressive Pseudo Bulbar Palsy strikes without warning. By the time it is diagnosed, a patient experiences great difficulty with normal daily activity, especially with chewing, swallowing, and muscle movement.

Helen lay in her bed unable to move any part of her body except her eyelids. The lines of communication between her brain and her muscles had broken down leaving her physically a prisoner in her own body. However, her mind was quite keen. She could express her needs and concerns by using the only part of her body that still responded to her brain, her eyelids. Those eyelids were her gateway to the outside world. Her eyelids were her voice, her signal that she needed some attention. If she was in pain, or thirsty, or hungry, or had an itch, or wanted to express herself, or needed anything whatsoever, it was her eyelids that did the speaking. Someone was always by her side: twenty-four hours a day, seven days a week, and 365 days a year—someone had to be in the room to hear Helen speak with her eyelids.

The routine was quite simple. You approached Helen's bed from her right side and asked, "Do you need something?" If she blinked one, long blink, that meant yes, and if she refrained from a blink, that meant no. This system worked most of the time except if she blinked when she intended not to and vise-versa. In this situation, you had to give Helen some time to compose her thoughts and regain her confidence. Encouragement on the visitor's part might add more frustration to the process, so it was best to give her the quiet she needed to concentrate on her particular need.

If she replied yes to your question, one long blink, you brought out the letter board, placed it in front of her so that she was able to follow your voice and your finger as you pointed to the letter. Beginning with the first word of her request, the visitor would ask, "Does the first word begin with a vowel?" If she blinked, you were on your way, and went down the row asking, "Is it an A, or an E, or an I, and so on until she blinked. You had to speak slowly and point directly at the vowel watching for any blink or near blink. The first letter could be a real challenge to someone who was not fluent in letter board.

If her request did not begin with a vowel, then you began to work across the second row of the letter board with the simple phrase, "Does the first word begin with a B, a C, a D, an F, and continue until the letter Z making sure that your finger was pointing at the exact letter you had voiced. Once the first letter was confirmed, you went on back to the beginning of the letter board repeating the same process. With careful attentiveness the first word of her request would appear. Then, you would write it down in the notebook and with confidence move on to discover the next word. Patience played an important part in this communication process since Helen often would confuse her letters if her vision was especially strained on any given day.

Frustration and disappointment often interrupted her train of thought causing tears to slowly trickle down her soft, pale cheek. One often had to show Helen the words she had constructed and allow her to continue or start again from the beginning. During difficult moments it was good to put down the letter board and remind Helen that it was okay to pause, especially when she experienced some anxiety. With perseverance, patience, and a willingness to allow Helen to speak her own words, a phrase or a request would begin to emerge like a ship approaching port in a thick fog. In some cases, requests would develop a pattern where often repeated words or phrases could be easily recognized, and a simple yes or no request could be posed.

For example, "Do you need something?" Helen would blink. The dialogue would continue, "Are you thirsty?" A blink, indicating a yes response to the question, would lead to the visitor, loved one, or a nursing home staff member carefully placing a few ice chips into her mouth since she was physically unable to swallow. Because solid food and liquids could be aspirated into her lungs and cause additional complications, her daily nutrition and hydration were accomplished via a carefully monitored feeding tube.

As with most of her needs, someone had to ask a yes or no question at varying times throughout the day and night. When

Helen needed to get the attention of her companion or anyone else, she would accomplish this by a rapid flicker of her eyelids or through basic human instinct. After spending some time with Helen, you could recognize the unspoken needs of a fellow human being, a real person who suffered the loss of expressing those needs verbally.

I walked into Helen's room and was greeted by a loud voice. "Glad you could make it!" Pat replied as she tucked the sheet neatly along the edge of the bed. Pat was Helen's best friend, spending days at a time at Helen's bedside seeing to her needs. She was an angel with the patience of Job who traveled from the Carolinas to the Washington D.C. area one week a month to be with her friend. "Helen's in a good mood. Well, she's in a good mood after we had our fight earlier this morning." Pat concluded with a hearty chuckle, smiled at Helen, and gently stroked her forearm.

Helen voiced her agreement with Pat's last statement with a sigh made audible by the trachea tube. A tear rolled down her face and dropped to the pillow. Her eyes caught mine as I looked up from where the tear had settled. I looked at Helen, and introduced myself, "My name is Matthew, and I'm the hospice chaplain." Helen looked at me, and then at Pat, and then blinked one, very long blink.

Pat smiled and said, "Helen likes you already. She is especially fond of men with beards. Isn't that right Helen?" Helen replied with one, long blink, and all of us chuckled. Whatever fears I had before entering the room had melted away with Pat's wonderful assistance. We continued to make small talk, and then Pat gave me the story of Helen's life and the progression of her disease.

Helen was born and raised in Connecticut. She attended college and graduated with a B.A. in English. She met her husband Michael, and they settled in the Washington D.C. area.

Although they had tried for many years to have children, they were unable. After careful consideration they adopted a young girl from South America named Emily. Soon after the adoption, Helen began to experience bouts of numbness in her limbs and an occasional loss of feeling in her hands.

At first, she dismissed these initial symptoms. But as they became more frequent and lasted for longer periods of time, she went to see her doctor. Tests indicated, supra-cranial fibrosis, a neurological disease that would result in complete physical debilitation. Helen, Michael, and Emily were devastated by the news. With time, they learned to accept the illness and physical limitations. Helen turned to her faith in God and to her church for some solace and comfort, while Michael and Emily sought the assistance of professional counseling. They decided that all care and comfort measures would be administered at home, for as long as possible.

As Helen's needs grew increasingly more demanding, for medical and financial reasons, Michael and Helen made the decision to transfer primary care to a nursing home. This decision, reached with much care and preparation, gave them an added level of safety and quality of care that could not be achieved at home. When Helen's diagnosis became a terminal one, of six months or less, both she and Michael agreed to have hospice helping in the final months of her life.

Throughout our hour together, Pat always deferred to Helen, and Helen always replied in her usual manner. Sometimes, she would blink when we expected her not to, just to give us a laugh, or as Pat said, "to keep us on our toes." Despite the adversity Helen was a real person with her own personality, sense of humor, and need to be loved and understood. Even in the face of such adversity, she still was in control of her life with the mere blink of an eye.

When Pat and Helen had finished, they turned to me and asked that I say a prayer. Pat turned to Helen and asked, "Do you want the chaplain to close with a prayer?" No blink. Pat laughed and I began to panic. Then, Helen opened her eyes very wide and closed them tightly clearly indicating one, long blink. I closed with a prayer and asked, "May I visit you on a regular basis?" Helen replied with one, long blink.

Few of us will ever experience her level of suffering or challenge in our lifetime. Some have felt the pain of a loved one in the grips of Alzheimer's disease or other forms of dementia. Others know the loss of physical movement and independence as illnesses worsen and loved ones are unable to care for themselves. But, a person, struggling with complete physical paralysis, while remaining mentally alert and totally dependent upon others for one's own survival, is faced with a seemingly impossible situation. Yet, Helen, her husband and her daughter, and a handful of dedicated friends seemed to have one-upped the illness. Any obstacles in communication between Helen and her family were overcome by love, patience, and a willingness to accept all that life offered. We all, together, mastered the communication routine quite well.

During the next visit, Samara, Helen's hired companion, greeted me at the door of the room. Samara was a young woman from Nigeria and had been working as a companion for people facing end of life for nearly five years. She was an instant hit with Helen and had been with her on the 7 A.M. to 7 P.M. shift for nearly one year. Samara possessed a special gift among workers in the health care industry. People trusted her instinctively. She seemed to have acquired an inner knowledge of Helen's wishes, needs, and insight into the deep spiritual issues that Helen had been wrestling with since the illness had left her completely incapacitated and dependent upon others. As a practicing Muslim woman, Samara prayed for Helen, and often the two of them prayed together for God's will to be done.

"Helen wants to speak with you. She is really upset about something and won't tell me why." As Samara spoke these words she shrugged her shoulders and added, "I'll be in the lounge if you need me."

I watched Samara leave the room, feeling a wave of uncertainty flood over me as I pushed aside the curtain and saw Helen, in tears, unable to regain composure. Like us she cried, but her tears were silent, and in the silence, more devastating than ones which come with loud bursts of emotion and volume. I approached her bed and gently took her hand in mine. I smiled and offered a quiet hello placing my free hand on her forehead and carefully stroked her hair.

She attempted a smile, but the tears kept falling, and I realized that some issue, that had been troubling her for some time, had made its way to the surface. Deep within my very being, I knew that a real challenge awaited me. Helen needed an answer or even some insight into a very difficult question.

As I reached for the letter board she exhaled through her trachea tube sending out an audible sigh. I stood by her side, and asked her if she was ready to begin. She blinked one long blink, and kept her eyes shut. A few seconds passed, although it seemed a very long time to me, and then she opened them again. I sensed a real change in Helen's disposition. Perhaps, she was tired of using the letter board. Her eyesight was not always reliable, and her bouts of confusion seemed more frequent. I placed the letter board on her bedside table and sat on a chair that was next to her bed. I leaned forward and asked her some questions outright.

"Helen, do you want to ask me a religious question?"

Helen replied with a long blink.

"Is the question along the lines of pain and suffering?" I asked.

Again, she responded with one, long blink.

"And why would God allow such pain and suffering to happen to anyone?"

My words seemed to hit the very core of her current struggle with the illness. Her tears increased. Her breathing became heavier. She looked deeply into my eyes, and I could hear her fervent plea for some answer to this question. I sat quietly for a moment and searched deep in my soul for an answer, not only an honest one, but also a compassionate one as well.

I began to answer, but then the words stopped. She looked at me, and I explained I felt her concern was worthy of an answer both well thought out and offered in a way leaving no room for guilt or second guessing. Right now, I was unprepared to offer an honest and accurate answer, but we could pray that the Holy Spirit enlighten both of us for this task? She blinked once, so we prayed.

Then I explained to Helen that my answer would be based on what I honestly believed in my heart as a Christian and what I knew to be true in many belief systems. All I asked was that she would give me one day to prepare so that my own shortcomings and weaknesses would not cause harm or create any panic in her life. She blinked one long blink to my requests. I picked up her Bible, and read Psalm 34. She seemed calmer, but had me promise to be back tomorrow with an answer. I blinked one, long blink, and she blinked back. We had reached an agreement; she would wait for my answer.

I arrived the next day at the nursing home. She had some visitors, so I briefly greeted her and her guests and told everyone that I would be back in an hour. I spoke to her briefly and said, "I think I have an answer to your question." She responded with one, long blink.

After I had visited with a few other hospice patients in the same facility, I returned to Helen. She was in bed, and alone except for Samara. Samara stood up as I entered the room and reassured Helen that the chaplain would have an answer so "she better listen." They both smiled at these words as did I. Samara patted me on the shoulder as she left the room, and I sat in a chair beside Helen. I looked into her eyes and asked, "Do you still want to hear what I have to say?" She paused and blinked. So I began to read.

"Every form of illness causes pain and suffering. Whether we are a little child with a runny nose and the chills hoping that mom can make us better or an elderly person lying in bed waiting for the time to be called home by our Creator, illness causes us to suffer physically, psychologically and spiritually. We soon discover the fragile nature of our human condition and realize that we cannot hold on to our life forever. The human body, as incredible and diverse as it is, is destined to slowly decline, deteriorate, and finally die. As a result an illness raises several inescapable questions: Why? Why me? Why now? What will happen to those whom I leave behind when I finally die?"

I paused. Helen looked and blinked. I continued.

"My Church understands the root cause of pain and suffering in our lives begins with our first ancestors, Adam and Eve. The Eastern Church views pain and suffering as a consequence of Adam and Eve's disobedience to God and fall from Paradise. Since God only creates good, pain, sufferings, and all things harmful or evil, are a consequence of that initial disobedience perpetrated by Adam and Eve. Pain and suffering are not to be considered a punishment for sin inflicted by God. Nor does the Orthodox Christian spiritual tradition understand pain and suffering to be a condition or essential prerequisite to pay for our redemption or salvation. St. Paul reminds us that, 'You have been bought with a price.' (1 Cor 6:20) Our redemption from sin and death has been accomplished by Christ's own suffering and death. We can share in his sufferings, but such acts should not be considered as the condition for our personal payment for the consequences of sin and death.

"When God declared to Adam and Eve the consequences of their disobedience, including pain, suffering, and death, (Gn 3:16–19), He did not act in a manner of punishing them. God merely names what will occur as a result of their disrupting the harmony between God and His beloved human creatures, and names the effect on them and the generations that follow. Illness, pain, suffering, and death become the legacy of the entire human race. Each of us inherits these infirmities even though we played no part in the disobedience of Adam and Eve. We suffer the consequences, but did not participate in its original cause.

"According to Eastern Christian thought, humans inherit not the sin of Adam itself, but the consequences. This differs greatly from Western Christian thought that follows the theology of St. Augustine which affirms the inheritance of the sin of Adam itself and the guilt as well. Cyril, the 4th-century bishop and saint of Alexandria, Egypt, summarizes the concept of why pain and suffering continue to this day: 'The multitude of human beings were made to share the consequence of sin not because they shared Adam's sin, they did not even exist yet; but because they shared his nature which had fallen under the law of sin.' In other words, they had departed from the original law of harmony and perfect communion with God.

"All of humanity is affected by our link to Adam. In the Gospel story of the Man Born Blind, (Jn 9:1–31), the Disciples ask Jesus, 'Who sinned, this man or his parents, the he should have been born blind?' Jesus responds, 'Neither he nor his parents sinned.' The passage clearly indicates that no link exists between the person's illness and the sins he might have committed. We are not punished by a God of vengeance for our sins with corresponding illness, pain, suffering or bad luck.

"For Christians, God is Love, and in love, there is no place for punishment. Nonetheless, as humans, we are inheritors of the consequence of sin: mortality, which translates into pain, suffering, and eventually death. Because of its material nature, our body is subject to illness. Physical, even psychological sufferings have no relationship to the individual or personal sin of the person afflicted with an illness. Pain, suffering, and death are inherent in our mortality just as love. Joy and happiness are also benefits of the mortal nature granted to us by God. We get both the good and the bad in our mortal package.

"So why is there illness, pain, and suffering? This is the question that many hospice patients and their families ask. It is the question you asked, and the answer to this question is as important to you and your family as the pain medication that brings you relief from your physical discomfort. It would help us to discover that sickness and suffering can take on a positive meaning in our life. It might sound strange at first to hear of an illness, especially a terminal illness, as something positive. Most of us view illness and suffering in a negative light. It can lead us to question the very foundations of our faith and even our existence.

"What positive fruit can an illness bring? Illness and the acceptance of our own mortality can decrease our attachment to a merely material basis for our being. We find that material wealth and worldly gains benefit us little. For many, we discover for the first time that our spiritual nature awakens and grows stronger as our physical strength diminishes and our bodies slowly accept their limitations. The great Russian author, Fyodor Dostoyevsky writes, 'A healthy man is always an earthly, material man . . . But as soon as he falls ill, and the normal, earthly order of his existence is disturbed, then the possibility of another world makes itself known to him at once; and as the illness worsens, his relationship with this other world becomes ever closer.'

"Illness and mortality turn some people toward God, reuniting us to God and drawing us closer to the real source of existence. It must be said, that some become disillusioned by suffering and lose all hope in God as a result of an illness. In every case, God speaks to us about salvation and affirms His will to help us attain life everlasting. We must accept His offer of help and join with Him in a concerted effort toward this goal. Like a physician who offers treatment for a bodily illness with a medicine or procedure that might cause additional pain and suffering, we must accept God's loving call to endure the bodily pain and suffering which can bring about the eventual goal of healing us spiritually.

"Illness, with its pain and suffering, continues to afflict us as a result of mortality, but this does not mean God has abandoned us. Jesus Christ, the second person of the Holy Trinity, participates in our suffering by His own suffering and death on the cross and ultimate victory over all pain and suffering at the Resurrection. Knowing that humanity left to its own ways could never see beyond its mortal existence, God chose to take on human flesh in the person of Jesus Christ. By this single act God's divinity is neither diminished nor does He take on sinfulness in his humanity. Jesus Christ remains Perfect God and Perfect man.

"Having taken on flesh and sharing in all human experience, except sin, Christ voluntarily suffers too, in the flesh. Humiliation, beatings, crucifixion, and death are accepted by Christ as a way to draw us closer to God. By His voluntary suffering and death, God shares fully in mortality in his human nature and remains fully God in his Divine nature. He takes on flesh that we might not suffer alone or believe that God has pre-ordained pain and suffering as punishment for creation.

"God takes upon himself all of humanity's pain and suffering in his human nature in order to demonstrate His ultimate gift of Himself, to remind us that all of humanity shares in pain and suffering as a result of our mortality, and that by sharing in our mortality, God shares our pain and sufferings while giving us also the possibility of sharing in eternal life with Him in heaven.

"His infinite love for all of humanity is expressed in the person of Jesus who accepts pain and suffering so that, in His Resurrection, we see vividly the promise of salvation and everlasting life. Jesus Christ, Perfect God and Perfect Man, opens up for us, all of mortal humanity, the path to immortality. As He suffered and gave up his life for us, so we, to a lesser extent, will endure some pain and suffering, succumb to death, giving up our life and thereby hope, for eternal life in heaven."

Again, I paused and allowed for the words to sink in. Helen looked at me, the tears still in her eyes. I asked her if there was anything that I said which caused her concern or was against the teaching of her own church. There was no blink. I asked again. She responded without a blink. I asked her if I could continue, and she blinked, one long blink.

"As we read any of the four Gospels telling of Christ's passion and crucifixion, we encounter his love, patience, and understanding. We can experience the wealth of forgiveness that He bestowed upon all of humanity—both believer and non-believer alike—while suffering the greatest of injustices, and eventually death. At the individual level, Christ responds to the repentant thief on the other cross, 'This day thou shall be with me in paradise.' Meanwhile, Christ extends forgiveness to all of humanity when he declares only moments before his unjust condemnation, 'Forgive them Father for they know not what they do.'

"C.S. Lewis takes up this in his work entitled, *The Problem of Pain*. Lewis captures the real essence of pain and suffering in light of the soul's spiritual wellness. He writes:

> I have seen great beauty of spirit in some who were great sufferers. I have seen men, for the most part, grow better not worse with advancing years, and I have seen the last illness produce treasures of fortitude and meekness from most unpromising subjects. I see in loved and revered historical figures, such as Johnson and Cowpers, traits which might scarcely have been tolerable if the men had been happier. If the world is indeed a vale of soul making, it seems on the whole to be doing its work.

"Our faith in God can grow stronger as an illness takes hold of the body, if we allow our soul to grow deeper in God's love, to enter into real communion with God. As we experience our own cross in the form of the pain and suffering caused by an illness, and if we can willingly accept that our mortal bodies will break down and eventually come to an end, then we can reap the spiritual benefits of the process. Our faith and resolve become stronger as we walk the path to Golgotha with our Lord. Patience finds itself at home in our bodies and souls when we accept the illness with love. Humility begins to burn brightly in our hearts as we accept the love that Christ offers from the cross. Repentance flows like a bountiful river offering a chance to seek forgiveness from those we have offended and offer it to those who ask.

"A terminal illness causes us to question the basis, the framework of our lives, including our beliefs, our system of values, our relationship with others and even life itself. It may prompt us to curse God or even to turn ourselves from Him. We must resist all temptations of pride and self-pity and urgently seek out the companionship of Jesus Christ, who suffered in the flesh, died and has risen, so that He might offer all of humanity a way to salvation and eternal life in the heavenly kingdom."

As I finished my answer to her question, I sat quietly and waited for a response. Her eyes remained tearful. I took her hand in mine and asked, "Does the explanation offer any understanding, Helen?" She blinked one, long blink, but a trickle of tears began to stream down her face. I wiped it with a tissue, and asked another question. "Are you hopeful but still frightened?"

She blinked again, and the silent tears continued to send a clear message that Helen was still struggling. She feared the uncertainty that awaited her and her family.

In the remaining days, we spoke about the unknown that awaits all of us. She was ultimately hopeful that God would indeed be there for her. Helen gradually overcame her fear of dying, though her tears were always a constant reminder of her love for those whom she would leave behind. Her husband Michael, her daughter Emily, and Pat were all there on that May afternoon when Helen's soul reached out and accepted the embrace of the loving arms of God, who welcomed home someone who had suffered as valiantly and lovingly as anyone before her.

Feeding Tube Worries

*"There are some things that you can only do with love.
You will know that you have love
when you do one of these."*
Walter Anderson, 20th century American Artist

"Papa, *yak vy spali?*" Paul, speaking Ukrainian, asked his father how he had slept that night. Ukrainian was the language that Papa loved to hear. He spoke English well, but Ukrainian was his first language, a language he loved to speak, and a language that brought him comfort. Since his stroke several years earlier, Papa was unable to speak in any language, but the sound of his mother tongue lifted his spirits in ways that very little else could do.

There was no response and Papa stared straight ahead into a private world where neither Paul nor I could see. Again Paul asked his question, "Papa, *jak vy spali?*" Papa returned from his private world and looked intently at Paul and me. This time he closed his eyes and shook his head from side to side. It was clear to all of us in the room that Papa did not sleep well that night. In fact, Papa had not had a good night's sleep for several weeks. As Paul continued to ask questions that Papa could answer by shaking his head from side to side for a "no" answer or nodding his head up and down for a "yes" answer, we discovered that Papa was in great discomfort due to the amount of nutrients and fluid flowing from his feeding tube into his stomach. Since the stroke, Papa had relied on a feeding tube for his nutrition and hydration. The stroke robbed him of his ability to swallow. Without the feeding tube, Papa would be unable to live for very long.

Yet, it was this artificial nutrition and hydration that was now causing the discomfort and congestion. When Papa took a deep breath or coughed, you could hear the fluid that had accumulated in and around his lungs. Papa grew weaker every day, and with each passing day, the amount of nutrients required by a person in Papa's condition also decreased. But there were no directives to decrease the amount of nutrients flowing from the feeding tube into Papa's stomach. Paul and his brother Simeon were determined to keep their father alive at any cost. What that meant, keeping Papa alive, would be the source of concern for Papa, his sons, and those involved with his care.

Papa came to hospice late in his illness. The struggle with end of life had been difficult on him as well as on his two sons. Both sons loved their father very much and simply could not accept the fact that Papa was dying. Meeting after meeting with the two sons, our hospice team, and the nursing home staff would start off and end with the same results. We would offer ways to make Papa's life more comfortable by decreasing the exceptionally large amount of nutrition and fluids from the feeding tube to a level more commonly prescribed for an elderly man confined to a wheel chair and facing end of life. The hospice dietician offered medical studies and advice on the amounts that a man in Papa's condition should be given to prevent the extreme congestion that made his life so uncomfortable.

At the conclusion of our meetings, Paul and Simeon, Papa's two sons, would thank us for our input and decide what was best for Papa. They would allow the rate and amount of the feeding tube to remain at its current level just in case Papa might rebound and gain some strength back. They would not accept the fact that their father was dying. One small miracle was their wish—their hope in light of Papa's declining condition and his doctor's diagnosis. At one meeting, Paul explained his reluctance to decrease the amount flowing from the feeding tube, "Papa is a fighter; he is a survivor."

Over the course of the next few weeks, I had a chance to speak with Paul and Simeon about their father. Papa was born and raised in the Ukraine. He graduated from the university with a degree in law and soon thereafter married his sweetheart. However, the tragic events of World War II forced them to leave their homeland and settle in a refugee camp in Germany during the war. Following World War II, the family found themselves refugees without a home. The Soviet Army had reoccupied their country making any return to Ukraine an unwise decision. Many refugees from the former Soviet Union who decided to return back to their homes following the war were labeled as traitors by Stalin's Government. Those who did return soon discovered this fact and realized their error much too late. Trainloads of refugees never reached their intended destination. Instead, the trains headed eastward into Siberia to the notorious prison camps know as the Gulag, a system of internal prison camps devised by the Communist government, where many millions perished.

Papa, his wife, and their youngest child, Paul, arrived in the United States and settled in Philadelphia. Surrounded by other Ukrainian families forced from their homeland by war and political upheaval, they prospered in their new community. They lived the American dream of owning their own home, a car, and a respectable place in society and among the Ukrainian-American community. When Papa and Mama were unable to care for each other, they relocated to the Washington D.C. area and lived with their sons. Mama passed away after a brief illness, but Papa remained with his sons in their home enjoying his retirement years as best as he could. He missed his wife and community back in Philadelphia, but realized that he would be unable to live alone.

"Papa grew up with all the horrors and depravity of World War I and the Russian Revolution." Paul quietly and matter-of-factly recounted to me on one afternoon. "He survived Stalin's carefully planned famine for Ukraine. He endured political upheaval, World War II, and those terrible German "relocation" camps. How can we now deprive him of his food?" In Paul's mind, Papa had survived the most terrible tragedies of 20th-century Europe, and he would not allow anything to prevent yet another potential survival story for his Papa. The feeding tube was their only hope. It would remain at its current rate until they thought there was no chance for their father to regain his strength and make another remarkable comeback.

∞

Paul and his brother's decision did not come as a surprise to us. Within the last twenty-five years, medical advances and technological breakthroughs have made it possible to maintain human existence for prolonged periods of time, even when there is little, if any hope, for a "comeback" or cure. Like Papa's two sons, many believe that a decrease in the amount of nutrients to a loved one on a feeding tube is tantamount to a slow death from starvation. The mere suggestion of a decrease in nutrients or hydrating fluids causes deep concern for many who do not fully understand dietary needs for those facing end of life. Feeding tubes can be real lifesaving miracles for many who suffer trauma or temporary disability whereby mechanical means of swallowing have become altered or shut down. But in end-of-life situations, they can serve the opposite function: they can prolong suffering and inflict greater pain and discomfort for extended periods of time.

These are difficult cases where a family is asked to make a decision to decrease the amount of nutrients that a feeding tube is providing to a loved one, or to remove the feeding tube completely. Hospice professionals and the medical community must address both the quality of life and the sanctity of life. If we wish to resolve the theological questions surrounding terminal illness and end of life, along with the moral and ethical ones, we must rethink the placement of feeding tubes. And we all need to determine for ourselves and our loved ones when to alter the amount of nutrients and fluids being prescribed for a terminally ill person.

Perhaps, we may have to decide whether or not a feeding tube should even be inserted into a terminally ill person, when that person can no longer perform and is not going to regain the normal bodily functions associated with chewing and swallowing. Since life is sacred and a gift from God, no one possesses the power to decide who will live and who will die. Such measures as euthanasia, physician-assisted suicide, and other means of ending life are contrary to Christian teaching and should never be employed.

Hospice upholds and honors the sanctity of life. It is the goal of hospice to journey with a terminally ill person as he or she approaches end of life and not to push them into an early death. Hospice provides the necessary physical, emotional, and spiritual support for a peaceful and hopefully painless end. Hospice shares the medical community's promise never to harm or neglect a patient as stated in the Hippocratic Oath. Yet in many cases involving a terminal illness, the question for all of us arises: "To what extent should medical technology be employed to sustain life and for how long?"

Age has nothing to do with the decision to place someone on artificial life support such as a ventilator or on artificial feeding. From an ethical standpoint, we need to acknowledge that at some point in the dying process, the withholding or gradual withdrawal of artificial life support may be morally correct. Each individual case must be carefully examined. Medical as well as theological guidelines should be used to determine whether artificial means of extending life, such as a feeding tube, will or will not serve as a means of regaining a quality of life. Will a feeding tube provide a temporary means of food intake until normal mechanical swallowing function returns? Once this has been decided, a feeding tube must be carefully monitored to determine the amount and flow rate a loved one is receiving. Too much fluid can cause unintentional harm, inflict greater pain and aggravate any physical ailment.

This process becomes increasingly difficult for those responsible for the decision or for loved ones who have decided on their own, as the end of life draws closer. Many of us will go to any measure to keep a loved one with us for as long as possible. The decision to decrease or even in some drastic cases, to remove a feeding tube, frightens us.

Food is a source of nutrition for the body, but food also represents the joy and bounty in life's special moments. All social events, whether secular or religious, have a central theme of celebration, and this celebration always includes food and drink. In many cases, we rent banquet halls and hire caterers to provide the best food money can buy. If we speak of religious celebrations, such as baptisms, bar mitzvahs, or weddings, a feast is usually prepared for guests to share in the joy of a particular religious rite of passage.

Around secular holidays, food plays a central role in the celebrations. Phrases such as "Fourth of July Barbeque," and "Labor Day Picnic," conjure up images of food, soda, beer—outdoor feasts at their finest. Food is not only essential to our existence; it is a central component of most celebrations. Ask someone to remove food from someone's life, and you can readily see how difficult it can be to make such a decision.

Such a decision is based on love and concern, the same love and concern that Papa's two sons had for him. However, their emotional ties were so great as to blind them to the harm the feeding tube was causing. To be able to ask ourselves how and why we are willing to keep our loved ones "alive" for the mere sake of living, we need to address the ethical and religious teachings as end of life nears. To assist us in these most difficult of decisions, the spiritual values we share are a necessary help.

Among health-care professionals in end-of-life care, there is a consensus that tube feeding presents many more risks than benefits especially in cases of advanced dementia associated with Alzheimer's disease. As we enter into the realm of medical advances the lines begin to blur. Tube feeding, ventilators, and other mechanical devices can prolong physical life, but serious dilemmas can result when these extreme measures are used.

Tube feeding keeps our loved ones alive, but what is the quality of life they now face? In the last decade a number of scientific articles published by medical professionals have determined that in terminal cases, where the patient is approaching death, dehydration and the withholding of food has a beneficial effect. Dehydration, for instance, stimulates the production of ketones in the brain. These are responsible for producing natural pain killers. In fact, a growing consensus in the medical literature indicates that "this normal form of natural dying is reasonably comfortable, thanks to the bodies own, endogenous analgesic mechanisms."

With a decrease in tube feeding amounts, patients facing end of life can actually die more comfortably and with more peace. As the body fluids begin to diminish, the person will experience a decrease in urinary output. Edema around the lungs as well as secretions to the lung will also decrease resulting in less coughing and congestion. Since there is a decrease in the amount of tube feeding, there is a decrease in the possibility that a patient will vomit the nutrients and fluid into his lungs and complicate his condition with aspiration pneumonia.

Real comfort for a terminally ill person can come through family members, friends, and trained volunteers. For example, by placing ice chips into a loved ones mouth or swabbing the mouth and gums with medicated solutions, we can provide increased comfort. It is comforting to the family to participate in a loved one's personal care and quality of life coming to a close, with small acts of kindness like this. Here we can see the Gospel come to light, "When I was thirsty, you gave me drink."

Careful monitoring of the patient, along with pain management, must accompany any decision to withhold artificial means of sustaining life. A patient, who is conscious and requests food or drink, must be obliged and their wishes granted. To merely sustain human existence for someone who is by all medical definitions, dead, can be considered immoral. If it is determined that a patient is brain dead—that cerebral and all brainstem function have been forever lost—then it is medically and morally appropriate to declare that the person has died. It is a drastic measure to completely withhold nutrition and hydration, or even take someone off an artificial respirator. These decisions should be implemented only when efforts to promote recovery have failed, and there is no evidence that any other efforts will bring the person back.

From a religious standpoint, the gift of life is sacred and must be preserved by all natural means. Human life, created in the image and likeness of God, is by its very nature sacred. A person's worth is not calculated in terms of value to society or productivity. All humans are of equal value at every stage of their life from conception to death. Quality of life, as seen from a religious perspective, can stand alongside sanctity of life affirming the belief that every person is equal.

Acting and feeling as members of one family, all of us are called to provide personal care, meals, and a comfortable environment for anyone facing end of life. In addition, we must address a person's social and spiritual needs in order to maintain a continuity of care that was enjoyed while he or she was at home. We also need to ensure the provisions of a morally, ethically, and spiritually beneficial environment for those approaching death.

In the liturgical services of the Orthodox Church, we pray, "For a Christian end to our life, painless, blameless, and for a good account at the awesome judgment seat of Christ, let us ask of the Lord." The people respond, "Grant this, O Lord."

This supplication sheds some light on the difficulties associated with health-care decisions that we often have to make for those with a terminal illness. First, we hear the words, "For a Christian end of our life." This phrase brings us squarely to the undeniable fact that we are going to die. Because death is a natural event in the life of every human being, no one can escape it, and so an end-of-life illness should be expected at some time in one's life. To merely extend biological life for the sake of living, without regard to quality of life and sanctity of life, is undeniably wrong. In cases like Papa's feeding tube, we find no evidence that a feeding tube prolongs life in patients with dementia.

We need not fear death. Rather we might set aside some part of each day to ponder the end of our life here on earth.

Our life is a gift freely bestowed by God, one day freely and willingly to be surrendered to Him, in order that he remains Lord and Giver of Life. We need to remember it is not ours to possess, but is His gift, and His choice to bring it to an earthly end. The call for us who journey alongside those facing end of life is to find more compassionate and spiritually beneficial ways to accompany our fellow brothers and sisters toward the final step of surrendering their life and future destiny into God's open and loving embrace.

We must not impose our own values and judgments upon those who are transitioning from this life to the next, but we can certainly assist them as they experience the sorrows and joys that come with an end-of-life illness. By engaging in this noble effort, we not only offer care and comfort to loved ones or friends who are approaching their final days on this earth, but we also reinforce our own understanding that death is a part of life. If we face this fact honestly and sincerely when our time comes, we will enter that "uncharted journey" with more confidence and understanding than if we had ignored the inevitable, or failed to be there for those who may have needed our comfort during their time of need.

The second phrase from the litany, "painless and blameless" addresses a concern that many of us will have when end of life draws closer. The church has always maintained that the medical community must do everything within its power to ease the pain and suffering of all persons. Each of us must do what is physically possible to assist others so that we will not feel guilt or be the source of blame, but to what extent?

Christian, Jewish, and Islamic clerics together recognize there is a fine line between comfort and assisted suicide. Artificial means of sustaining life are recommended only to ensure a quality of life that falls within the boundaries of the sanctity of life.

Under careful medical supervision, a decision to decrease artificial nutrition and hydration does not contradict the religious teachings of most monotheistic faiths. In severe cases, where a loved one has been declared "brain dead," the removal of artificial ventilation is also permissible according to some faiths, provided the family or medical power of attorney has agreed.

When loved ones are terminally ill, most of us will employ any means possible to keep them with us for as long as possible. Yet there comes a time when they will eventually die. Preparation for our own "terminal phase" can be an important contribution of the life of the patient and family or friends. We need to inform ourselves and our loved ones about the real facts of sustaining life beyond the "normal" limits—limits defined by the medical community and guided by our religious or spiritual beliefs.

Why My Husband?

*"Suffering is not a part of the brain. It is a
part of the mystery of being human."*
Daniel P. Sulmasy author of The Healer's Calling

Pete and Katherine sat on a small padded bench outside his
room. The nursing facility where Katherine and her family
decided to place Pete was one of the best in the area. As
Katherine once told me with a smile, "It is certainly one of the
most expensive."

Katherine continued to talk to Pete in the same loving way
she had prior to his illness. "Hey old man, who do you love?"
He looked confused and said nothing. "Hey old man, I'm talking to you. Do you hear me?"

A smile came to his face. For some reason, he heard the
voice, a familiar voice, and he turned toward his wife and replied,
"Yeah." The smile on Pete's face turned into a grin.

With some reassurance that her husband truly recognized
his wife, Katherine asked again, "Who do you love, old man?"

He looked at his wife and said, "You."

It might have sounded like a question, but it did not matter. She threw her arms around him and kissed him square on
the lips. He said nothing else, but he kept smiling. For 63 years,

Pete and Katherine have been a team. They had met at a dance while Pete was on leave from the Army during World War II, were married at the local Catholic Church, and bought a home just down the street. They had been faithful members of their church, never missing a Sunday mass or holy day of obligation.

Now Alzheimer's disease and dementia had interrupted their life. Pete no longer recognized his wife as readily. Katherine was often frustrated. Sometimes she felt resentful. Above all, she was growing angry at God. She blamed God for the illness. In a phone conversation with me one day, she asked a question that many of us in her situation might ask, "How could God let such a terrible thing happen to such a good person like Pete?" There is no easy answer for that question.

When Pete was first diagnosed with dementia, it seemed hardly noticeable. He seemed to forget the little things. However, with each passing day, Pete became more forgetful, and was now unable to remember his own name. Katherine continued to attend church when she could, but found little comfort in the service. She became cynical in her approach to worship. The priest's words of faith and hope seemed hard to believe. The Gospel was no longer alive in her life. She could not find the comfort and peace that faith provided before the illness. Her faith seemed to have vanished almost as slowly and imperceptibly as Pete's memory had.

On one afternoon, I met Katherine at the nursing facility. She was in the dining room, feeding lunch to her husband. She had taken over this duty some three months ago. The staff at the facility had noticed he was no longer capable of feeding himself. He had not lost his appetite, just the ability to move the fork from the plate to his mouth. There is no escape from Alzheimer's—even the most basic of tasks are rendered impossible by this disease.

Katherine looked up and announced to Pete that I had come to visit. He seemed unable to hear as he continued to concentrate on his lunch. Each spoonful was eagerly consumed. I said hello to Pete, and he looked at me without saying a word. He had no idea who I was. Katherine smiled and asked me how things were in my parish. I told her that the parish was doing well. Then I asked her how things were in her life.

"I think that I'm reaching my limit. Pete loses a little function every day while I lose a little of my faith every hour," she said with some haste as she grabbed the glass of juice that Pete's arm was determined to knock over. She placed the glass out of his reach and picked up the fork in order to continue with feeding him lunch. Pete watched the movements of his wife with some interest. A smile appeared on his face, which raised Katherine's spirits as she sat next to him, fork in hand; ready to feed him another helping of carrots and peas.

I looked at her, and asked, "What gives you comfort? What brings you peace of mind?"

Katherine set the fork down and thought for a moment. She stared at the plate and then said, "Being alone. That gives me the greatest comfort. I just cannot stand to be around large groups of people, especially in church." As she finished her sentence, a few tears came to her eyes. She brushed them away and picked up the fork ready to give Pete another helping of mashed potatoes.

We sat quietly for a while as Katherine continued to feed Pete. I broke the silence with a suggestion. "Why don't you change the way you worship. Perhaps you can go to the small chapel attached to your church where the Blessed Sacrament is kept. It's usually open during the day, and most likely there will be no one there to bother you. Most people who visit that chapel want to have some dialogue with God, in a private way."

The words seemed to float in the air for a while. Katherine smiled politely and said, "I'll think about it."

A few days later, I checked my voice mail at work. Katherine had left a message. "Matthew, I went to the chapel yesterday. I sat for a while. I cried. I got really angry at God, and I think He heard me. I'm going back to the chapel today after I feed Pete his lunch. I want to hear what He has to say. Thanks. Your mom should be very proud of you."

∞

The phone clicked. It was a brief message, but a good start. Healing is difficult, especially the first step. For Katherine, as well as for most of us, confusion hits when an illness or a calamity befalls us. Our faith in God is questioned. We aim our eyes heavenward and ask, "Why me, Lord?" Our feelings become muddled in the panic and uncertainty, especially of a terminal illness. When a loved one enters the final weeks or days of life, we often have mixed feelings about God and His presence in our lives. Anger, jealousy, rage, and even fear seem to grip our souls leaving us helpless as we desperately seek some answer to unanswerable questions.

Katherine's faith in God had been shaken. Faith in God is a relationship. All relationships, whether they are between individuals, corporations, or governments, are based on trust. Our relationship with God, too, is based on trust. If an event or crisis alters our trust in any way, the relationship becomes uncertain. Our relationship with God can be altered tremendously if we experience some crisis or event that adversely affects us or our loved ones such as a terminal illness. We may turn to prayer for an answer, but a prayer unanswered can lead to further doubt about our relationship with God. This uncertainty might manifest itself in confusion, anger or outright resentment toward God.

When a patient or family member tells me of their anger or confusion with God, I reassure them that this response is normal, especially in times of crisis. Rabbi Harold Kushner, in his book, *When Bad Things Happen to Good People*, offers a very healthy approach to pain and suffering. When he speaks with men, women, and children who have suffered some tragedy in their life, he sees a pattern among them. They usually ask two questions. First, why does God cause suffering? And secondly, why did God allow this to happen to me?

Rabbi Kushner challenges us to look at these two questions from a very different approach. He asserts that God is not the source of suffering. God does not cause pain, suffering, and misery in this world. There is some reason for tragedy in this life, but it does not stem from God's will. Rabbi Kushner finds some insight into this most pressing question in the words of the Psalmist, the Prophet David. "I lift my eyes up to the hills; from where does my help come? My help comes from the Lord, maker of Heaven and earth." (Ps 121:1–2) It is in these words that we know precisely the source of our help, the Lord, Who is not the source of our pain, suffering, and death.

God does not look down from heaven and choose who will die a painful death or who will suffer unjustly. God is not a micromanager in everyone's daily life. God does not choose our movements or control our thoughts and speech like a puppeteer. But somehow, God gets the blame. If a tragedy strikes, such as a tornado, flood or other natural disaster, everyone from the news reporters on the scene to the survivors and even the insurance companies place the blame squarely on God. Often you hear the phrase, "An act of God" to describe some catastrophic event.

We can get angry at injustice or suffering without blaming God. We can support those who suffer, who reach out for help, and in so doing, remain a player on God's team. Our expectations need to be re-evaluated, not our trust in God.

Many of us are taught that God hears our prayers, and all we need to do is let Him know of our needs. In time, He will see to our needs. Here we can see that our expectations might be unrealistic. As a chaplain I know that God can handle our emotional change of heart. I advise my clients that they need to voice their concerns, doubts, and feelings about God. Scripture reminds us that even those closest to Christ had some difficulty understanding how God works.

The Apostle Peter denied that he knew Jesus Christ at a time of great crisis (Mt 26:57–76). During the interrogation of Christ, several bystanders approached Peter accusing him of being one of Christ's followers. Three times Peter denied that he knew "the Man." When he heard the rooster crow, Peter remembered the words of Christ's prediction, "Truly I say to you, that this night before the cock crows, you shall deny me three times." Peter was overcome with grief. Peter had lost his faith. He no longer trusted in the Lord. A crisis had forced him to make some serious decisions.

His relationship with Christ was altered, but not broken. Christ continued to trust in Peter even though Peter had strained the relationship. Peter prayed and received forgiveness. Christ's love is infinite, we all need to understand and accept this in our relationship with God. The love God has for us is the source of the love we share with one another. Out of God's love, Peter was forgiven and became a leader in the Christian Church.

Like Peter, some of us may lose faith, even if just for a moment. He repented and received the mercy of God. The relationship was broken, but not severed. We must try to follow this example. If we lose faith, if we lose heart we must not despair. It is then we need to find our quiet place, a side chapel where we can pray and commune with God in peace. Our thoughts, our feelings, and our actions must be given time to realign with God's presence in our life. The relationship needs repair. God is waiting for us with faith and with love. All we need is an open heart willing to trust in the Lord.

Midwest Practicality

"For in self-giving, if anywhere, we touch a rhythm
not only of all creation, but of all being."
C. S. Lewis

Working in Washington, D.C. offers an exciting opportunity to see and experience the nation's Capital City at both its finest and not-so-finest moments. One of its finest moments is spring and the arrival of the cherry blossoms. This event alone is worth the effort to navigate through the endless lines of automobile traffic and swarms of tourists that clog the tidal basin in late March and early April. If you go early in the morning, before 8 A.M., you can get a really spectacular view of the entire tidal basin bathed in a sea of pink blossoms set aglow by the rising sun. In the late afternoon, when the tourists head back to their hotels for dinner, I head to the tidal basin with picnic blanket and basket in hand, and sit amid the sea of pink. It is at these times that I can really feel God's presence in the cosmos.

I also find God in the compassion, concern, and self-sacrifice of our patients and their families. Rarely do you find family members who are unwilling to give all of their effort to care for and offer comfort to a loved one facing a terminal illness.

Driving across the 14th Street Bridge leaving behind the image of God's presence among his creation, the cherry blossoms,

I head toward a retirement facility just beyond the beltway in Virginia. This particular facility, an elegant retirement home, offers independent living quarters as well as step-down care for those who need assisted-living and nursing-home care. It was not the first time that I had been to this facility. Hospice sees about a half dozen patients in the nursing-home level as well as in the patients' private apartments.

The majority of the residents in this facility have lived in and around the Capital area for most of their lives. Upon entering the building, you will find a few of them sitting in the solarium, which resembles a hotel lobby with elegant couches and stately wing backed chairs neatly arranged around coffee tables. Brass lamps fitted with stylish lampshades rest on highly polished end tables showering a pleasant glow and warmth over the room. Newspapers and other reading materials are neatly arranged on the coffee tables in front of the chairs and sofas offering the residents a chance to sit and catch up on the news in and out of the facility.

No one can pass through the lobby without one or two friendly hellos from the residents seated on the chairs and sofas. This is usually followed by pleasant conversation, remarkable insights about life, all from these venerable elders. They possessed a wealth of knowledge about Washington, prior to and during World War II. They recounted amazing stories of our nation's Capital during the war. "President Roosevelt loved to drive in his fancy automobile with the top down and wave to us as we walked to work or strolled about the city," one resident recalled for me.

Often, their stories recalled the rapid growth of the city. Incredible building projects dotted the city and surrounding region. Like mushrooms following a healthy spring rain, the buildings sprang up around the city. "The Pentagon was completed in less than 18 months, and Tyson's Corner was just a mere crossroads with a general store," replies another resident who decides to join our impromptu gathering and moves her wheelchair closer to us. Life is filled with memories, and these wonderful people have plenty of memories. By the way, Tyson's Corner is now a six-lane road that boasts some two miles of malls, shops, and other business outlets.

I thank them for their brief history lesson and continue on my way through the lobby, past the front desk, and down a long corridor to my intended destination, the apartment where Mary and John lived. They had just moved there in early February having spent most of their married life just a mile or so down the road in a home purchased in the late 1940s. Having researched the area looking for a comfortable place to retire, they decided on this facility. "Mary can find a bargain before the advertisement makes it to the newspaper, "John said quite matter-of-factly as he continued to explain how and why they moved to this retirement home. "She has always been good with finances, and that's been all right by me. I just don't have the knack for that sort of business."

John paused as his wife slowly made her way into the living room. Diagnosed with advanced lung cancer just a few weeks before my visit, and having received news from her doctor that the cancer had spread to her spine, Mary remained fiercely independent, alert and in complete control of her plan of care. Her husband assisted her only when she called upon him to do so. She insisted that we meet in the living room and not in her bedroom though it meant she had to expend an incredible amount of energy, enduring some painful moments as she maneuvered out of her bed and walked to the living room.

It was my first visit with them under hospice care, yet both of them greeted me with a certain familiarity. We exchanged pleasantries, and before I could direct the conversation to reasons why I was in their home, Mary quickly assumed the reins and directed the discussion to a topic of great concern to both of them.

"Matthew," she said as if she had known me for a long time, "we've never been much for church or organized religion. In fact, we haven't been attending any regular church for I don't know how long." She paused and adjusted her oxygen tubing. She had recently agreed to use the oxygen as breathing on her own became more difficult. Although it meant she lost some of her independence, she adjusted the nasal canula, the part of the tubing that divides into two smaller tubes and supposedly fits comfortably in one's nostrils, in such a way as to remind us and the machine that she was still in charge. Her Midwestern charm and fiercely independent spirit had not been dulled by the cancer. It had only been softened, while still maintaining a politeness and respectability often found among her generation.

"So now you know where we stand with church attendance and the like," she said, "but we still want to have a proper service and burial when I die. I'm not sure when that will be, but John and I decided before you arrived that you should be the one to perform the service."

As Mary finished her sentence, I glanced over at John. He was sitting on the couch next to his wife, silent, attentive to the conversation, and in complete agreement with his wife. They were a cute couple sitting on the sofa. Both of them, small in size and somewhat private people, possessed a tangible desire for creativity. One only had to glance at the walls of their apartment and see Mary's oil paintings and John's framed black and white photographs neatly hung to realize how these two individuals had come together and created a life as one. But, there was no visible sign of affection: no hand holding, no hugging, no sweet kissing, not even a tearful acknowledgement of

Mary's pronouncement of her impending demise. Yet as I watched and listened to these two Midwesterners, born and raised with a no-nonsense approach to life, I began to understand that love can spring from sheer contentment with life and with one's achievements.

As I continued to visit Mary and John on a routine basis, I learned a lot about their unique relationship as husband and wife. They were both raised in Wisconsin by parents who traced their ancestry to Denmark from where their forebears had emigrated in the mid-19th century. These immigrants embodied the ideal of the Protestant work ethic. Honesty, integrity, courage and faith were not simply virtues in a book; they were the foundation of one's existence. The entire spectrum of well worn proverbs and homespun advice formed the basis of daily life. Say what you mean and mean what you say. Always keep your word. It is not polite to let everyone know your troubles. Hard work never killed anybody. Be forever cheerful. Always respond to questions about your own well being, whether good news or bad, with a simple, "I am fine. And how are you?"

With this advice, repeated throughout their childhood and teen years and combined with hard work, both Mary and John had achieved more than their parents' generation could have imagined. During their life together, they had both landed government jobs in Washington, raised a daughter, sent her to college, and saw her married to a good and faithful man. Having lived the American dream and reaped the harvest of their efforts and energies, both John and Mary retired with comfortable pensions and a good amount of savings. Although they never talked much about death or the dying process, they knew that one day they would confront the issue. Now, faced with Mary's impending death and fully immersed in the mid-stages of the dying process, they accepted death as a part of the entire master plan of life.

On one of my visits, Mary came into the room with a puzzled looked on her face. She sat down in her usual place on the sofa and took a deep breath with the assistance of the oxygen concentrator. Since she had agreed to this concession, Mary's quality of life improved as she went about living life and doing what she enjoyed. With the oxygen by her side, she and John could venture to the dining room for a meal with friends and not have to worry about Mary becoming fatigued or short of breath. Although she was facing end of life, she did not have to surrender all of her joys. A free and uninterrupted flow of oxygen enabled her to continue as normal a life as someone in her situation could hope to have.

As she regained her composure, she looked at me and said, "Matthew, I have been wondering about one issue so I want you to tell me something about your religion. I mean what does the Orthodox Church teach about end of life?" Her question was not merely a curious notion. When Mary asked a question, you knew she had spent some time preparing for an answer that would settle the issue. She was serious about end of life, especially hers, and I could perceive that she was searching my mind for an answer that might satisfy her skeptical view of most religions on the subject of death.

"I'm really glad you asked me this question since the Bible study at the parish has been discussing this same topic. The answer to your question is a bit complicated, but if you give me a chance, I just might offer some insight and understanding into end of life. Perhaps the best way to view the Orthodox Church's understanding of death is to think of our life on earth as a book. Our current existence, life as we are now living it, represents the preface of our story. It serves as an introduction to what will be the body of the book—life after we die.

"The moment of death signifies a starting point of the main story. As we know, death is a certainty, but it is also a mystery.

All of us can be sure that we are going to die. If we focus our efforts to avoid this inevitable event in our lives, we will lose out on a life filled with living. When we learn to accept our mortality, the undeniable certainty that death will come, this acceptance liberates us and grants us the freedom to live life to its fullest.

"The understanding of death as a certainty is balanced by another: death remains a mystery. Gather together all of the greatest thinkers of all the different religious traditions, and you will discover that we know very little about death. In my opinion, it is St. Paul who best describes the process we call death. He reminds the Christian community in Corinth to remember death as a continuing process: 'I die daily.' (1 Cor 15:31) The entirety of the human race experiences this daily death since all living beings die a little each day. Our earthly journey, the preface to the book of our life, encompasses a series of little deaths as well as little births. Each night when we fall asleep, we experience a death, and when we wake up the next morning, we experience a birth in our awakening from the night's sleep. Since we do not fear this normal pattern of sleep as we expect to arise the next morning, perhaps we could direct our efforts toward our final falling asleep, the sleep of death, in a similar manner.

"The Orthodox Faith understands death as an expected event. Also present throughout life, death is actually foreign to God's original plan of creation. Reading in Genesis about the Biblical story of creation, we find that God did not plan on death. God is good and a loving Creator who wills only good. He takes no pleasure in destroying since He created all things to live. It is impossible for evil to proceed from God since God is infinitely good. So when God created Adam and Eve, the first man and woman, He did not include death in that creative process.

"The Orthodox Faith draws this understanding from the Patristic tradition, a collective body of oral and written history that began with the Apostles, and continues to this very day having as its basis holy scripture. This tradition states that God as Creator never intended death, nor the polarity of mortality and immortality. God allows human freedom to stop at mortality (mere death) or to aspire to and achieve eternal life."

I paused a moment as Mary turned to her husband, and then back to me, and asked; "So Adam and Eve had a choice from the very beginning. They could have been just like God, in the sense of being immortal, if they had not eaten the fruit from the tree in the Garden of Eden?"

"In one way, the answer is, yes." I replied, and then added, "But the immortality Adam and Eve might have achieved would not be equal to the level of Divine Immortality. They would never achieve equality with God, but would share in the Divine gift of immortality. There was a choice for Adam and Eve. God did not coerce them. Rather He warned them, 'For in the day that you eat the fruit from the tree, you shall surely die.' (Gn 2:17) Death entered into man's existence through the sin of disobedience; the human race died a spiritual death at that moment of Adam and Eve's disobedience, a separation from God in a mystical sense. Only later did physical death, the soul's separation from the body, occur.

"St. Paul's Epistle to the Romans reinforces this important point. 'Through one man sin entered the world, and through sin came death, and hence death spread to all men.' (Rom 5:12–13). On the day when Adam and Eve sinned, that is their disobedience to God, they died spiritually, and they also lost any possibility to achieve immortality. They began to experience pain, suffering, and undergo the natural process of aging and eventually physical death."

John looked at me as he sat on the couch and spoke in a very soft and humble tone. "So your church does not believe that God punished Adam and Eve, and the rest of us with death. In other words, God did not curse the human race with death as a form of punishment for Adam and Eve's sin and declare the rest of us guilty by association."

"That is correct." I replied. "Death, as the Orthodox Church understands it, is not a punishment by God, but the fruit and result of Adam's sin. Death is seen as a separation or withdrawal from God, the source of life. The very illnesses that you and I suffer, for that matter, our daily aches and pains, came about as a result of Adam and Eve's decision to disobey God. Disobedience translated into separation, and separation led to our physical death. In some instances it takes 70, 80 or 90 years for the physical death to finally arrive, but all of us undergo a slow decline of our bodily systems until the day we die. The certainty that we are going to die is a reflection of the fact that we are living in a fallen world. No one can escape this process. It is a part of our living."

John poured some water into a glass and placed it in front of me. We sat quietly for a moment. Mary looked at me and said, "So your church claims that God hasn't punished all of us because of Adam and Eve. We're just born into a world that guarantees death for all of us. We are born, we try to live good lives, we undergo the aging process as our bodies slowly breakdown, and we call you folks in when we have six months or less to live." Mary smiled and her grin became contagious as we all had a good laugh.

"That's my Mary, always looking at the practical side of things." John chuckled as he repositioned himself on the sofa, folding his arms across his chest. "But can you tell us what happens at the moment of death? What does your church teach about this realm of the unknown?"

Sitting before this couple I just wanted to jump up and give them both a hug. As we at hospice like to say, "They are just the cutest." But that was not a part of their lifestyle. John had told me once that his relationship with his wife was much like any other part of their life. There had been very little affection throughout most of their 50-plus years of marriage. During one visit, he told me that he could not remember the last time they had kissed. Nonetheless, they loved each other very much, had dedicated their lives to each other and their daughter, and would find strength and courage in this accumulated life of memories.

Their relationship offered them a wonderful opportunity for learning in their journey of life, for discovering who they were, and in a very odd sense their definition of true love. We tend to think of marital relations based on a certain amount of affection and sexual compatibility. Romance, adventure, and excitement seem to be the prescription for curing many ills that often plague relationships. We are bombarded on a daily basis with advertisements for adventure, romance, and excitement that are guaranteed to "put that spark back in the relationship." For Mary and John, their secret to a successful life together rested on old-fashioned compatibility that had very little of what we would call the romantic spark.

In fact, as word of the illness arrived from the doctor, there was no stream of tears followed by long embraces and words of consolation. They expected death to come one day, and neither of them believed they would be spared the suffering and pain that goes along with the dying process. Now, Mary and John wanted to have some answers about death. They needed these answers so that they could move on in their journey without fear or apprehension. In their world, these unanswered questions represented the missing pieces to the puzzle of life. When they found the pieces and placed them into the puzzle, a spiritual peace would enter their lives. Any anxiety over separation or loss would be diminished by knowing that the journey would continue.

"The point of death for us occurs when the soul leaves the body." As I spoke these words Mary and John assumed a serious look. I continued the explanation, "As I mentioned earlier, we call death a mystery since events that take place at the hour of our death and events that immediately follow cannot be understood completely. Humans are psychosomatic beings, meaning both the soul and the body constitute the whole person. Death occurs when the soul departs from the body.

"The separation of the soul from the body is a temporary event. It is an intermediate state, for they will be united again at the Second Coming of Christ. The soul therefore does not die. It does not simply disappear, nor is it reincarnated into other bodies. Every body is connected with one soul, and every soul is connected with one body. As the soul prepares to leave the body, an angel, in some cases your Guardian Angel, the one given to you just after conception when the soul is placed into the body, arrives to take you to one of two places: the place of refreshment, Paradise, or the place of torment, Hades.

"This part of the dying process is what we call the initial judgment since at the final judgment, or more commonly called the Second Coming of Christ, the soul will be united again with the body and then all will be judged to receive the Kingdom of Heaven or be resigned to Hell. But at the initial judgment, the righteous and the sinners are lead to their proper places. The righteous live a comfortable and free life in heaven with the angels and God in the paradise from which Adam and Eve fell. They bask in the glory of God. The sinners are sent to Hades and live with affliction and inconsolable grief like those condemned to sit in prison and await future judgment.

"The Orthodox Faith holds that our souls do not actually travel to a physical place since the soul which leaves the body does not act through the senses. Paradise and Hades are places beyond sense and comprehension. We should view these two places as particular modes of life, two ways of being by which we can partake of the glory of God or find ourselves completely cut off from it. At death the soul travels to a different dimension. It is through God that the souls of the righteous are aware of their condition and ours: they hear us; they receive our prayers and pray to God for us. They are able to do all this by God's grace that is their unity with God."

"Okay, stop right there." Mary interrupted as a small grin took hold of her face, communicating that her abruptness was well intentioned and not malicious. "This is the part that confuses me. How do they hear us? And are they able to communicate with us?"

Mary's questioning gave me a chance to take a quick drink of water. As I reached for the glass, I noticed John's look of approval and unspoken advice to drink deeply since there would be more explaining to come. John possessed a remarkable gift of facial communication that offended no one but informed anyone willing to listen.

"Communication" I replied, "between the living and the dead begins with prayer and the sacramental life of the Church. Any notion of communicating with the dead through mediums, tarot cards, Ouija boards, or the magic eight ball is contrary to Orthodox Christian teaching. As we read in the lives of the saints, occasions do happen when the dead directly communicate with the living in dreams or in visions, but this occurs through genuine prayer, on the spiritual level. It is not in Madame Cleo's crystal ball that our communion with the departed is known, but in prayer and the celebration of the Eucharist. As we pray for them, they pray for us. It is through this mutual intercession that we and they are joined in a mystical union rooted in faith and in love.

"As to the doctrinal or scriptural basis for our prayer for the departed, we simply answer 'with faith and with love.' We pray for the dead because we love them. We certainly do not pray for them because God might neglect them without our prayerful reminder. God loves all creation, and with our prayers for the departed we unite our love for them with God's love for them. Death does not mean they cease to exist. Whether alive or dead, we are all members of the same family, and therefore we intercede for each other. Physical death cannot separate the bonds of mutual love and mutual prayer that join us in a single unity.

"Of course, we do not understand exactly how prayer benefits the departed. When we offer prayers for those still alive, we cannot explain how this intercession assists them. We know from personal experience, and the testimony of others that prayer is effective. Whether offered for the living or the dead, the efficacious nature of prayer remains a mystery. We cannot comprehend the relationship between the act of prayer, the free will of those for whom we pray, and God's grace in all things. As we pray for the departed, we are comforted that our prayer encourages them to seek God's love, to desire God's will as our own, and to remain forever alive in Him.

"If we change the way we speak about the dead, we might be able to change our attitudes toward the dead. Too often, we speak of our departed loved ones in the past tense. While conducting memorial services for hospice patients whom I have had the privilege to serve, I always refer to them in the present tense. Life is a journey, and our time on this planet is relatively brief. When we depart this life, the body dies while the soul continues the journey waiting the day of final judgment. Once, following the burial of a particularly well-loved father and husband, the entire family stood by as the daughter thanked me for reminding them that their father was still alive, just living in another dimension of space and time. I could not have agreed more.

"Of course, this does not erase the experience of grief and loss caused by the death of a loved one. However, by using the present tense, we can alleviate anxiety and ease some of our grief. Often we postpone seeking reconciliation with someone whom we have alienated, offended or who has offended us. Death intervenes before we have forgiven each other. With great disappointment we are tempted to think that it is too late, there are no more chances, and nothing can be done.

"On the contrary, we can offer up prayer and speak directly to the departed loved one or friend using the same words that we would employ had they still been alive, as if we were meeting them face to face. We can ask their forgiveness. We can remind them of our continued love. From that very moment the relationship changes as our hearts inform our entire being that a fresh start has begun. The slate is clean.

"This is how we communicate with the departed. I truly believe that our prayers not only help them as they continue their journey, but also help us work through our grief and loss. Just as it is comforting to hear others say they will remember us in their prayers while we are still living, the same holds true for the departed. In the Orthodox Church, we believe in the power of prayer at all levels, and those who have departed this life are not outside the realm of its beneficial effects.

"There is a story based upon the writings of Christian monks and nuns living in the deserts of Egypt during the fourth and fifth centuries. One day a hermit monk was walking across the desert and came upon a human skull. He looked at it and began asking questions as to who he was and where he was following his death. The skull replied that he used to be a pagan priest and was now in Hades. He explained that Hades is an awful place where people are bound back to back and unable to see the face of their neighbor. Loneliness, isolation, and hopelessness fill their existence. But when someone prays for them, a divine light penetrates the darkness, and they can catch a brief glimpse of their neighbor. This one act brings them immeasurable joy, comfort and some hope. As a pastor, I find the prayers for the departed a comfort for those who have asked for them as well as a reminder that one day I too shall be on the other side awaiting prayers on my behalf.

"Overall, death is a blessing. Although it was not a part of God's original plan of creation, it is His gift, a sign of His mercy and love for creation. If we humans lived forever, trapped in the vicious cycle of sin in this fallen world, it would be a fate too terrible for us to imagine. So God has given us a method of escape. Like a rail yard worker uncoupling two connected train cars freeing them from one another to be linked at another time, God uncouples the union of soul and body, so that He may shape them anew on the day of Judgment. He is like the potter described by the Prophet Jeremiah, 'So I went down to the potter's house, and there he was working at his wheel. And the vessel he was making of clay was spoiled in the potter's hand, and he refashioned it into another vessel and it seemed good to the potter to do.' (Jer 18:3–4) God, the Divine Potter, lays His hand on the clay of humanity, spoiled by sin, and He breaks it in pieces, so as to fashion it anew according to its original glory."

I paused. Both Mary and John looked intently at me. Mary began to fidget with her oxygen tubing. After she finished adjusting it she said, "Well I like what you said. It makes some sense to me, and I hope that you'll tolerate us long enough so that you can perform my memorial service. No church, mind you; just some family and friends from this place in the small chapel downstairs. And go ahead and wear your black robe. I've seen photos in *National Geographic* of Orthodox priests, and I like what I see. I also look forward to hearing some prayers on my behalf no matter where I might be after I finish this part of my journey. You've managed to chase away most of my doubts, and I feel a whole lot more at peace with the whole process."

Mary's health slowly declined. Yet at our weekly team meetings at hospice, her nurse, and in my opinion, an angel of mercy would simply say this about our patient, "God bless her—she really knows what she wants and more importantly what she needs." I couldn't have said it any better. Mary passed away not in the midst of uncontrolled pain, or uncertainty or fear, but on her own terms. Like so many times throughout her life, Mary was still in charge even at the moment of her death. The disease did not win; it did not rob her of life. It was Mary who made the decision to leave this world when she had finished all that needed to get done.

Two months after I first met Mary, I performed her memorial service in the chapel on the first floor of the retirement facility. It was packed with more people than John or Mary could have ever imagined. He thought twenty might show up, but by the time the service began over 50 people filled the chapel. Chairs had to be set up outside the chapel to accommodate the overflow. Mary, with her Midwestern no-nonsense style, her homespun charm and witty humor, had touched so many people in just the four months she had lived there.

After the service, John, his daughter and her husband, and I drove to the cemetery where Mary was to be interred. It was a beautiful spot situated near a large pine tree on the edge of a hill. Mary had gotten a good bargain when she bought that plot those many years ago, and one she would enjoy for many years to come.

Vanessa's Dream

"It is not by faith that you will come to know Him,
but by love; not by mere conviction, but by action."
St. Gregory, Pope of Rome

"Matthew, I had a real scary dream last night." Vanessa spoke with clarity and authority. For nearly five years she had been sick, battling HIV/AIDS and the complications that arise as the disease progresses. To say it wasn't easy living with the disease and all the stigma associated with HIV/AIDS was an understatement. Initially, family and friends kept their distance. Vanessa felt alone, almost abandoned. Suicide was never an option, but the initial loneliness and isolation struck deep into her psyche. Her son's father was serving time in prison, and Vanessa hit rock bottom. Each day became a marathon of emotional hurdles while any hope for a positive outcome seemed very distant.

Fortunately, her family worked through the first shockwaves of the diagnosis. They learned to accept Vanessa for who she was and not simply a person with an incurable illness. In talking with her mother, I discovered that love is truly the most powerful force in the world. "Chaplain, I looked at her and my grandson and knew their place was with me." Her mom smiled. It was a smile that only a mother can manage when there seems little hope on the horizon. Her eyes welled up with tears, and so did mine.

That was nearly five years ago. Things had changed. Vanessa was living in an apartment with her mother and eight-year-old son, and she needed answers to recent events in her life. She understood how and why she contracted her illness. She was grateful that her son did not have the virus. But she wanted to know the meaning of her dream last night. "It was like I was asleep and awake at the same time." Again Vanessa spoke without hesitation.

Prior to this dream, her responses to my questions were short "yes" or "no" answers. Sometimes she would respond with a shrug of the shoulders. Often, I would simply sit with her as she watched her favorite soap opera or afternoon talk show on TV. I would try to find the right moment to ask her a question that might open up a discussion about her illness. Most of these attempts produced little return. In fact, I do not recall any time at which she initiated a conversation or took a real interest in my attempts at providing spiritual care.

Vanessa was not a religious person. She attended church with her grandmother when she was a youngster, but by age 13, she decided that church was simply "uncool." Prayer, the Gospel, and Jesus Christ had not played an important role in her life for nearly ten years. Yet, at 22 years of age, this young woman, loving mother and now terminally ill person had just begun to explain to the chaplain an event that she could have never imagined occurring before her illness.

"I know it was Him. It had to be Jesus." She said with a hint of excitement in her voice. "He was dressed in white, and the light surrounding Him almost blinded me. I got scared. He opened his arms real wide, but He didn't say anything. I know that I'm going to die soon, but I wasn't ready last night. So I ran from Him. I ran so fast that I woke myself up right here in this room. I must have yelled or done something because my voice woke up my Mom. She's been sleeping in this room with my son and me since my sickness has gotten worse."

Vanessa paused for a moment to catch her breath. I looked at her as she sat on the edge of her bed. She was wearing an extra long tee shirt that draped over her emaciated body like a sheet over a floor lamp. Her last visit to the doctor indicated that she had lost over 50 pounds in the last six months. She now weighed a little over eighty pounds, and for the past two weeks, she had not eaten any food except for bits of dry toast and some ginger ale.

She was still hungry, but the HIV/AIDS medication made her nauseous. Unable to keep any food down while she took her medications, she decided to stop taking her pills in an attempt to satisfy her hunger. She hoped this brief halt to her medications would allow her to regain some of the weight she had lost, and give back some lost strength too. Vanessa would stop taking her medication for a week, keep some food down, and then return to taking her medications. This plan did not help in any way. As she resumed her medication, the nausea would always return, and she would be unable to eat. She continued to grow weaker with each passing day.

Her mother tried to improve Vanessa's appetite by making her daughter's favorite meals, but the disease had overtaken her immune system. She remained in a constant state of nausea. Only small sips of soda along with some ice chips taken throughout the day gave her any break from the constant pang of hunger that gnawed at her weakened body. Hour after hour, and day after day, Vanessa sensed she was losing the battle with her disease.

Vanessa looked up at me, and asked, "So what does it all mean? Did I do the right thing by running away from God? Is He going to get mad at me for not going with Him?" She heaved a deep sigh and then coughed. Although she expressed little emotion about her illness to me before today, the dream had struck a deep chord in her soul. She had just experienced a profound visitation, a near-death experience in her own mind. To her, it was both real and a dream. More than ever, she sought some answers to the spiritual dilemma that now confronted her.

I looked at her as she sat on the edge of her bed. Her head was slightly bowed in front of her. I asked myself, "How do I approach this explanation." She was 22 and the mother of an 8 year old boy, but on many levels, she behaved like a teenager happily ignoring people and events around her. Was she in deep thought or just taking a rest after telling me about her unsettling occurrence? She knew that she was dying, but she wanted a little more time to finish the work that remained.

I gently called her name. She responded to my voice with a slight startle. "Vanessa, God is not angry at you for running. It wasn't your time." My voice trailed off quietly like a warm breeze on a hazy summer afternoon. It was a welcomed response, refreshing, but short lived. I waited for her reaction.

A single tear began to roll down her check. She attempted a smile, but was interrupted by a very violent cough. As she regained her composure, she smiled and replied, "Thanks. Thanks for believing me. I get real confused now, so I need to get some things straight in my head. It's all happening way too fast."

I took her hand in mine. We offered a silent prayer that seemed to last for a very long time. It was only a few moments, but it had a wonderful calming effect on Vanessa. The silence was broken by the hospice nurse. She was carrying a new tray of medications neatly arranged in the weekly pill box. Vanessa and I smiled as the nurse began to explain how and when to take the medication. Vanessa would take the pills, not because they would help her, but because it was just the thing to do.

I gently squeezed her hand. It was a gesture of reassurance that she had done the right thing. She wasn't ready, and God understood. She looked into my eyes, and I heard her silent response: the next time He appeared, she wouldn't run.

∞

We hear many stories from our patients and their families about strange events taking place as they face their final day. Some patients may experience visitations from Jesus, the Virgin Mary, or some being they simply call "God." Others may dream about departed loved ones and speak directly with them. Still others may tell of an "out of body" experience, describing the strange sensation they felt as they seemed to be in a dreamlike state, yet completely aware of their surroundings.

These events, which I refer to as end-of-life phenomena, are not uncommon. As the final days approach and the soul prepares to leave the body, many inexplicable events are taking place. From a Christian perspective, the soul's departure from the body is a traumatic experience. When a person realizes that death is near, a host of emotional and spiritual issues often surface. Doubts arise about how one has lived life. Guilt, fear, uncertainty and even anger can enter the picture. Loved ones begin to question the meaning of their own lives while at the same time preparing to leave this world.

As patients wrestle with the emotional and spiritual issues, some begin to experience dreams, visitations, and visions. With these end-of-life phenomena, patients might begin to question their ability to discern between reality and an imagined event.

Family members and friends also question if these events are real or hallucinations. In every case, a chaplain, a friend, or a loved one must address another person's experience without any preconceived judgment. We all must deal honestly and respectfully with these experiences, perhaps offering a reasonable explanation as to why this extraordinary event has occurred. For most of us involved with the care of a terminally ill person, this is not easy.

There are several instances when these phenomena are most likely to occur: with a clinical death, with someone approaching death, and sometimes when drug addiction is involved. In the first case, an individual's heart stops beating, respiration has also stopped, and the person is pronounced "dead." This clinically "deceased" person experiences some extraordinary event. The individual seems to be floating above his or her body while loved ones stand around the bed and grieve over the death. The same individual may encounter a figure in dazzling white or an angelic figure. Following some brief period of time, the person returns back to the body, regains a heartbeat and breathing resumes. In some cases, the newly departed awakens immediately, and to everyone's surprise, begins to talk about their recent "out of body" experience.

A more common experience is found among individuals who are approaching death or are "actively dying." The phrase "actively dying" describes the finals hours of an individual's life, when the heart rate and breathing are barely noticeable. They are aware of their condition and able to describe events that are taking place. Finally, where drug addiction is involved, a patient may experience some end-of-life phenomena. One needs to be honest and loving to those with a history of drug abuse using great caution to distinguish between hallucination and "real-life event."

Within the context of Christianity and other monotheistic religions, there is a large body of literature that deals with end-of-life phenomena. Historically, the Christian Church has maintained a cautionary approach toward individuals who experience visitations, out-of-body experiences, and dreams as death approaches. Yet, it does acknowledge that some experience near-death phenomena. We know the accounts of many, both saints and sinners, who have come back to life and described what they saw, and these testimonies have had a great impact on their lives, the lives of their loved ones, and on society as a whole.

The surprise and astonishment experienced by today's society with such phenomena stems, in some part, from the fact that the modern world has forgotten the existence of life after death. Some people believe that a person's life ends with the end of the biological life. Viewing existence in rational terms only, they are amazed when they discover "the other world." They hear of these after-death and near-death stories, and stand in awe and wonder.

Yet, we only need to examine the Biblical accounts of resurrections from the dead to offer some insight into these end-of-life phenomena. In the Old Testament, the raising of the son of the widow in Zarephath of Sidon by the Prophet Elijah (1 Kgs 17:17–24) illustrates one after death experience. More well-known accounts of resurrections from the dead are found in the New Testament. Jesus Christ raises the son of the widow of Nain (Mt 2:1–10), the daughter of Jairus (Mk 5:1–5), and the most well-known account is the raising of Lazarus (Jn 13:1–34). In each of these accounts, none of those raised from the dead explain what they experienced or who they met. Their experience was faith-based, a belief in God's love and mercy, so we as modern-day observers need to explore the events that occur in the lives of those around us.

Like Vanessa, many people at the moment of death or when they come back to life after death, have seen very remarkable and strange happenings which cannot be explained in a rational, scientific manner. Faith cannot be scrutinized under a microscope or on an x-ray. Real discernment is necessary in order to validate a loved one's experience. In this realm surrounding end-of-life phenomena, we are guided by the epistle of John the Evangelist who advises, "Beloved, do not believe every spirit, but test the spirits, whether they are of God." (1 Jn 4:1).

The testing of spirits is another way of defining the process of discernment, and within the entire Christian Church, a great tradition gives rise to discernment. If one is able to discriminate between a real experience, one coming from God, or a hallucination, one originating from demonic fantasy, Satan, then one is able to find some meaning in a particular event. The ability to distinguish these two sources of near-death phenomena is the ability to discern what is truly good and what is opposed to good. This gift of discernment stems from one's own spiritual life, one's spiritual development, and directly related to the person's current spiritual health.

In the case of Vanessa, we discover a young woman who has lived a life contrary to her own Christian background. However, in her search for spiritual peace as end of life approaches, she discovers deeper truths about herself and her relationship with God in her near-death experience—her dream. Although no one can accurately know any other person's spiritual life, we can see that Vanessa is searching for her way back to God. As her disease progresses, she appears to be growing spiritually stronger even though her body is growing weaker.

A spark of faith reignites her spirit. Her desire to draw nearer to God has diminished over the years, but never gone out. Within her heart, she hopes for a change even within the short period of time left to her. She has experienced a profound event in her life, wants some explanation, and deserves an answer honest and respectful.

Men and women who have lived Godly lives often possess the gift of discernment and are able to tell whether a visitation is Godly or demonic in nature. For most of us, this work of discernment is a difficult task. We need to turn to our clergy, elders, holy men and holy women, to those gifted with the gift of discernment, to offer some meaning to end-of-life phenomena.

I have tried to show how difficult it is to evaluate patients' experiences in their approach to the end of life. One way to discern the origin of end-of-life phenomena is to examine the fruits of such experiences. For example, Christ teaches his Disciples how to test these spirits. "By their fruits you will know them. Every good tree bears good fruit and every bad tree bears bad fruit." (Mt 7:16–17). So, we novices need to examine the fruits or outcomes of these experiences. If after a vision peace and calm prevail in the heart, it is a sign that it came from God. However, if it creates turmoil and agitation, it is a sign that it came from Satan.

A dream, a visitation, or out-of-body experience can help bring about profound changes, even as we approach the end of our lives. As a result of her dream, Vanessa no longer saw death as a violent break in her earthly existence. She saw an opportunity to live life and accomplish those things that she had not done thus far. Work still awaited her, and so she was given the chance to "run back to her room." God, our loving God, offered her a chance to change her life, and she chose wisely. The month that remained brought opportunities to grow in faith, in love, and in spirit with her mother, her son, and those who loved her most.

The whole truth about dreams, visions, and out-of-body experiences is not confined to science journals or the handbooks of psychologists. Spiritual in nature, end-of-life phenomena ought to be tested for their source of origin. Some people approaching death perceive a new reality for the first time. We think that the life we see is the real life, but beyond the sensible and perceptible, there exists another world unhampered by human reason and senses. It is in that reality beyond where the region of uncharted territory awaits those approaching death. End-of-life phenomena often help guide the dying person toward the real goal of our journey in life, the authentic home for the soul.

Everybody dreams. The messages in our dreams are signals from the sub-conscious to the conscious. Dreams often communicate vital messages and in some cases, can make a profound difference in our lives. Recognition of their importance allows doors of perception to open; we can begin to live life more fully, acknowledging the signs that life is coming to an end.

Vanessa was not ready to die. She needed a sign, or perhaps permission to continue on her earthly journey for just a little longer. Her dream was not a hallucination or some fantasy. It was real. Her dream gave her the strength and courage to continue for another month, taking care of unfinished business, and helped her live more gracefully into dying and beyond.

Epilogue

Anyone involved with the care for the terminally ill knows the weight of demands and needs of the patient and the families. End-of-life care can be the greatest challenge that patients and their caregivers may ever face. The suffering, the pain, and the uncertainty in the lives of those involved can be overwhelming. Spiritual care, delivered with love and compassion, can provide true healing as our loved ones, friends, or even strangers seek peace in their journey of living into dying.

Almost anyone can be a compassionate and caring spiritual-care provider. Whether we are professionally trained health-care workers, ordained clergy, or individuals who wish to make a positive difference in the final days of a life, all possess the tools necessary. We can all contribute to spiritual care capable of healing. I recall one visit to a nursing home when I asked the elderly man how often he prayed. He replied, "At least twice a day because that's when the cleaning lady comes in, takes my hand, and offers a few prayers with me."

A quiet touch and a gentle smile may be enough to communicate the message of faith, hope, and love. When spiritual concerns arise, we need to deal with them honestly and lovingly. Our approach to those in search of an answer to a spiritual issue ought to address their need at that moment.

Spiritual care should never be used to coerce a patient or family member in a manner inconsistent with their beliefs or wishes. That could be more harmful than the terminal illness. We need to be mindful of our own limitations in the realm of spiritual care. From health-care professionals to family and friends, all are called to contribute compassionate care, each with his or her particular gift. Part of compassionate care includes spiritual care, and spiritual care is necessary, as every human being is also a spiritual being.

We are all united to one another on this planet. The final days of our life should not be spent in pain, in confusion, or in turmoil. We should be able to make our loved ones' final days painless and peaceful. The medical community provides the pain medication to relieve the physical suffering, and together we can all provide the spiritual care to bring spiritual and emotional healing to the terminally ill in their final days.

No one possesses all the tools when it comes to caring for the terminally ill. All of us have a responsibility. All of us possess particular gifts for compassionate care for the dying. As medical resources and training attend to pain management, spiritual and emotional tools are necessary and available to meet the spiritual needs of the terminally ill.

No one deserves to die in pain, loneliness, anger, or confusion. Together, we can provide spiritual care that brings peace at the end of our journey in life. Make the most of your days. Offer yourself, your presence and your care for those who are waiting to meet you.

Acknowledgements

I would first like to thank Paramount Market Publishing for its support. The president and editor, Doris Walsh, and publisher, James Madden, provided their expertise and kindness throughout the final stages of the process.

I want to thank Mary Bolles for her expertise in preparing the manuscript for publishing. Her kindness, generosity, and friendship brought additional joy to this project.

A special thanks goes to Susan Wick, who took the time to review the draft manuscript. Her input was invaluable, and I pray her labors yield fruit one-hundred fold.

I want to thank my wife, Katrina, for her endless support and encouragement throughout my writing of this book. And I want to thank my son, Tony, for his patience and understanding.

Finally, I thank the patients and families whom I have served. It was an honor and privilege to serve them in their time of need.

Appendix 1

A Brief Guide to Spiritual Care

The following provides a brief summary of spiritual concerns associated with end-of-life. Patients and families may find answers to their specific needs in the scriptual verses and in the explanations that follow. All biblical quotations are from the New King James Version of the Bible.

Spiritual Concern:
Presence—Simply being there

Scriptural Reference:
    Old Testament—Ps 51:17
    A humble and contrite heart God will not despise.
    New Testament—Jn 19:25
    Now there stood by the cross of Jesus His mother, His mother's sister Mary—the wife of Clopas, Mary Magdalene, and the disciple (John) whom he loved.

Patients are always aware of another person's presence.
Patients need to know someone is there.
Presence brings comfort.
Presence is a gift that says "you matter."

Spiritual Concern:
Presence—Developing a relationship

Scriptural Reference:

Old Testament—Pr 11:14

Where no counsel is, the people fall; but in the multitude of counselors there is safety.

New Testament—Rom 12:10

Be kindly affectionate toward one another with brotherly love, giving preference to one another.

Patients and families must get to know you.

Patients and families need to trust you.

Patients and families will rely on you once a relationship has been established.

Spiritual Concern:
Presence—Learning to listen

Scriptural Reference:

Old Testament—Ps 46:10

Be still and know that I am God.

New Testament—Mk 4:24

Take heed what you hear with the same measure you use, it will be measured to you.

Patients and families need to be heard.

Effective listening instills trust and respect.

Listening opens up the heart and the mind.

Spiritual Concern:
Presence—Words that harm

Scriptural Reference:
Old Testament—Pr 15:1
Grievous words stir up anger.

New Testament—Mt 12:36
Every idle word men speak they will give an account of it in the day of judgment.

Patients and families do not need trite expressions or quick fixes.
Avoid statements that are unrealistic or impossible.
No answer is a good answer.
Find an appropriate answer in consultation with others.

Spiritual Concern:
Presence—Words that heal

Scriptural Reference:
Old Testament—Pr 10:13
On the lips of him that has understanding wisdom is found.
New Testament—Mt 8:8
Speak a word, and my servant will be healed.

Patients and families need to hear honesty with compassion.
Patients and families need realistic answers to complex issues.
Healing is not a cure, but it is the start of a new journey.

Spiritual Concern:
Purpose—Prayer

Scriptural Reference:

Old Testament—Ps 5:1

Give ear to my words, O Lord.

New Testament—1 Thes 5:17

Pray without ceasing.

Prayer brings comfort to patients and families.

Prayer communicates the needs and concerns of patients and families.

Prayer can be done in private or with others.

Prayer is often the "first line" of defense that patients and families have.

Spiritual Concern:
Purpose—Life is sacred

Scriptural Reference:

Old Testament—Gn 1:26

Let us make man in our image according to our likeness.

New Testament—1 Cor 12:27

Now you are the body of Christ.

There is a balance between quality of life and sanctity of life.

Every life has value in that it is made in God's image.

Every life has meaning.

Spiritual Concern:
Purpose—Pain and suffering

Scriptural Reference:

Old Testament—Lam 5:1

Remember, O Lord, what is come upon us; consider, and behold our reproach.

New Testament—Jn 9:2–3

Who sinned, this man or his parent. Jesus answered, Neither.

Pain and suffering exists in this world as a result of fallen humanity.

Everyone has pain and suffering including the righteous and the saints.

Patients and families can realize some good from the pain and suffering in the long run.

Spiritual Concern:
Purpose—Patience and Persistence

Scriptural Reference:

Old Testament—Jb 1:21

The Lord gave, and the Lord has taken away; blessed be the name of of the Lord.

New Testament—Jas 5:10

Take the prophets as an example of suffering, affliction and patience.

Patients and families need to rely on you for strength.

Spend more time with patients and families.

Emphasize their strengths and try to provide tools for improvement.

Care-givers and hospice staff need proper rest and quiet time.

Spiritual Concern:
Purpose—Honesty

Scriptural Reference:
  Old Testament—Pr 12:17
    He that speaks truth shows righteousness.
  New Testament—Jn 8:32
    Be truthful in all things.

    Honesty with compassion is the rule.
    Respect the wishes of the patient and family.
    Offer healing that brings closure; don't promise miracles.

Spiritual Concern:
Purpose—Keeping an open mind

Scriptural Reference:
  Old Testament—Pr 31:9
    Judge righteously and plead the cause of the poor and needy.
  New Testament—Jn 8:11
    Neither do I condemn you; go and sin nor more.

    Focus on the person not the illness.
    The history of the patient and family is just a part of the
      story.
    No one is in a position to make moral judgment on
      anyone.